IN THE ABSENCE OF THE EMPEROR

Also by Simona Pakenham

Ralph Vaughan Williams:
A Discovery of his Music
Pigtails and Pernod
Sixty Miles from England

SIMONA PAKENHAM

IN THE ABSENCE
OF THE EMPEROR

LONDON – PARIS
1814–1815

CRESSET PRESS
LONDON

First published by
The Cresset Press
2 Clement's Inn, London WC2
Printed in Great Britain by
Western Printing Services Ltd, Bristol

For

Phil and Ferdre

List of Illustrations

Contents

Contents

CHAPTER I

Europe at Peace Again

PEACE. PEACE. PEACE.
A large assortment of
TRANSPARENCIES
designed by the finest artists,
for the present glorious occasion,
to be lent or sold.
J. Lawley's, 20 Blackfriars Rd.[1]

So ran an advertisement towards the bottom right-hand side of the personal column of *The Times*, under the appeals for men-servants, healthy wetnurses and cashmere shawls for exchange. The transparencies were for private use or for display in shop windows with a light burning behind them. They were smaller versions of the great ones that drew crowds into the London streets the same night—Monday, April 11th, 1814—and for the rest of that joyful week. In the Strand, Akermans were exhibiting a transparency of 'the Corsican attacked by Death, with appropriate emblems';[2] on Old Swan Stairs, over Messrs Carrat & Sons, a portrait of the late Mr Pitt looked down, with the quotation 'England by her firmness has saved herself, and by her example is Europe saved.' The front of Carlton House was wreathed in orange lamps, their festoons framing the illuminated names of Austria, Russia, Prussia and England, with the motto 'Vivent les Bourbons' in the centre. Above the architrave a transparency floated showing the Genii supporting the crown of France over the name Louis XVIII. On Ludgate Hill, Blades, Glass Manufacturers to the Royal Family, outdid all its rivals with 'a superb transparency' in which the Emperor of Russia and the King of Prussia, in a chariot drawn by four horses, and led by the figure of Fame, entered Paris, while Peace flew down from the sky to crown them with laurel. 'On the side of the victors was a fine likeness of the illustrious Blücher, attended by a horde of Cossacks; old men, women, & children, were on their knees, imploring blessings on their Deliverers, while others were strewing the road with flowers and olive branches; two fine female figures in a kneeling posture, offered each Sovereign a mural crown; and in the streets an immense crowd appeared with flags of their legal king. In the background was the triumphal arch of St Denis, erected in honour of Louis XIV; and at a distance, a high pillar broken, with the statue of Buonaparte falling to the ground.'² Above this fantastic picture was a bust of 'the victorious Wellington' wreathed with laurel. Mottoes were everywhere, 'Thank God' on Pulteney's Hotel in simple lights; 'Good Old Times' under the name Ferdinand on the Spanish Ambassador's residence, 'a phrase selected with peculiar felicity'¹ as the reporter of London's principal newspaper remarked; 'Moscow burned—Paris spared' over the Foreign Office; 'The Reward of Perseverance' on Lord Liverpool's house; 'Vive le Roi' on that of the Prince de Condé in Lower Berkeley Street. Adams in Fleet Street was excessively wordy—'Magnanimity has overcome tyranny. The Scourge of the human race is fallen; his military career like the hour glass is run. Russia! thou hast our praises! Prussia! Austria! & Sweden! Ye have done your duty; & England! your virtuous efforts will resound from Pole to Pole! Thy fame will endure till Time shall be no more.

Peace! Peace! was thy leading star; universal Peace shall be thy reward.' The largest crowd in Fleet Street was drawn to the offices of the newfangled Gaslight Company which had put up a tree of laurel leaves with a profusion of blossoms, each blossom being a jet of the strange new flame. 'Their keen and quivering splendour threw every other into comparative obscurity.'[1]

Miss Mary Berry went out to see the illuminations on the Tuesday. She was not impressed with anything but Carlton House, the Horse Guards and the Admiralty, but she did not penetrate to the city or see the gas lights. It was exactly a week since she had noted in her diary hearing the news of Napoleon's defeat. She took Lady Hardwicke, who was in the house with her when it came, straight out to call on her old friend Madame de Staël. They found her completely overcome, 'no arguments, no reply, no wit; she showed true feeling for what she always calls her country.' Albertine, her daughter, was also powerfully affected. It had been a week of amazed conversations, everybody pinching themselves to be certain they were awake, 'the struggle was over—not *faute de combattans*, but *faute de quelque ennemi à combattre.* Nobody could talk of anything [else].' That Sunday had been Easter Day and the whole of London had gone into the parks to walk about in the bright sun, drunk with the universal gaiety, talking to strangers in an un-English manner, 'unable to take in the idea that we were already at peace.'[3]

On that same Monday, King Louis XVIII, (as he had styled himself since the death of his nephew the Dauphin), brother of the murdered Louis XVI, took his dinner in public at his country retreat in Buckinghamshire. Hartwell House, where he had lived for the past five years, and where his wife had died, was beseiged by several thousand of the residents of Aylesbury, Stanmore and the neighbourhood. It had always been the custom of the kings of France to dine in public and no distinction was made among the ranks of persons admitted to walk round the table and observe him eating. Louis, who at nearly sixty was immensely fat and much troubled by gout, had a prodigious appetite that was little affected by the ups and downs of fortune. On this day of rejoicing he sat down to dinner at five with the Duke of Gloucester, who had ridden out to bring congratulations from his brother the Prince Regent. The weather was fine and the park full of people wearing the white cockade of the Bourbons.

The news had reached Louis, as it had reached the British public, somewhat piecemeal. He had already received a deputation from Dunkirk begging him to return to France. His brother, the Comte d'Artois, 'Monsieur', was on his way to Paris in the wake of the Allied conquerors. Stories of Napoleon's abdication had been uncertain and contradictory, but now his removal from France had been settled. The great events of the previous week were briefly summed up in a letter from Thomas Sheridan to Samuel Whitbread, the brewer and Member of Parliament, 'Bonaparte has signed his resignation—Bourbons proclaimed—Victor, Ney, Marmont, Abbe Sièyes, Caulaincourt, &c, &c, &c, have signed. The Emperor has a pension of 200,000 per ann.; and a retreat in the Isle of Elba. . . '[4] In common with most Whig opinion in Britain Samuel Whitbread rejoiced in the moderation that had been shown by the conquerors. 'A limited monarchy in France, with Religious Liberty, a Free Press and Legislative Bodies such as have been stipulated for before the Recognition of the Bourbons, leave their Restoration without the possibility of Regret in the Mind of any Man who is a Lover of Liberty and a friend of his kind. Paris safe, Bonaparte suffered to depart, after the experiment has been fully tried of effecting a peace with him, upon such terms as he was mad to reject—'tis more than I dared to hope.

'Then the great example set of the Fidelity of all his Generals, and of the Armies they commanded, up to the very moment he himself gave up all for lost and opened his own Eyes to the consequences of his own desperate Folly, must surely have its effect on the World, and redeems many of the Treacheries Men have committed against their Leaders. I confess it pleases me beyond measure... God grant us a long and glorious Peace.'[4]

Whitbread's humane and moderate attitude to the fallen Emperor was far from being reflected in the anti-Whig newspapers and would have commended itself little to the celebrating public. *The Times* compared Buonaparte (spelt thus) to Robespierre for cowardice and described him in various articles as 'a little dirty hypocritical villain' and 'a Monster, a Tyrant, an Assassin, a Robber, a Liar, a Hypocrite'.[1] *The Gentleman's Magazine* summed up his fall as 'distinguished by pusillanimity and hypocrisy', 'what he had done through fear, he wished to have it thought proceeded from a love of the French nation... His character presents a strange mixture; of which perfidy, obstinacy, cruelty, arrogance, ambition, and pusillanimity, are the leading features. Had his soul possessed its boasted Roman virtues, he would not have survived the disgrace by which he had been overwhelmed; nor become the Pauper of those whom, in his days of prosperity, he treated with the most audacious arrogance and unwarrantable insult.'[2]

The public, less sanctimonious in its triumph, enjoyed a week of Guy Fawkes-type jubilations. On Monday, Sir William Curtis, Bt., supplied beer and ale to the citizens of Southgate, and provided clothes and decorations for an effigy of Bony to be burnt on the green. On Wednesday, the watermen and youths of Richmond, disguised as Louis and the Allied Sovereigns, made a procession through the streets. Everyone who could not rise to a costume wore a lily or a white cockade. The fun spilled over into the next week when Wanstead 'celebrated with plentiful libations of porter', three thousand of the 'lower classes' rejoicing over another burning of Bony in 'perfect harmony and order'.[1] The richer people of Yarmouth subscribed seven hundred pounds to give a dinner of roast beef and plum pudding on the quayside to 4,000 of the poorer ones. The crowds in London, in the parks by day and in the city by night, continued to be enormous. Everyone was struck by their good order. As Miss Berry said, 'The crowds in the streets were in the best possible humour, and there was neither accident, difficulty, nor confusion in any place.'[3] The Hon. H. G. Bennett, M.P. wrote to Creevey, 'It is pleasing to see so many happy faces.'[4]

In the course of the week other signs showed that the peace was real. Prisoners-of-war were being landed at the ports. Orders to regiments about to embark for France were being countermanded. Four packet boats were already plying between Calais and Dover and the Comte de Gramond had brought over the flag of truce in one of them. Communications were about to reopen between Brighton and Dieppe. The channel had been closed to the travel-loving English for more than ten years and they had felt hemmed in. All over the country people were making plans for a spring or summer holiday abroad.

Though the nation was in a festival mood, private griefs and tragedies continued in their accustomed way. Fanny, Madame d'Arblay, had the rejoicings spoilt for her by the loss of her beloved father, the composer and musicologist Dr Burney, who died at Chelsea College on April 12th. Fanny had married a French emigré and had gone with him to Paris after the Peace of Amiens in 1802. The couple had been caught there when war broke out again a year later and had been forced to spend the next ten years in France. Fanny had eventually managed to return to England, through the good offices of a member of Napoleon's government, using her father's age and ill health as a pretext, though an even stronger motive for her wish to leave France was fear that her young son Alexander would be conscripted into the Emperor's armies as soon as he was old enough. The prospect of a Bourbon restoration and of reunion with her beloved Monsieur d'Arblay would normally have sent her into a transport of joy, but Fanny was a person who took family bereavements unusually hard and she was quite prostrated with sorrow.

Private sorrow was the constant background to the life of the Royal Family, to whom Fanny Burney had been, till her marriage, a much loved lady-in-waiting. She had been at hand to watch the gradual progress of the King's strange illness and had had, as she confided to her diary, a most affecting encounter with him in Kew Gardens some time after he had been declared hopelessly mad. For some years now the King had been kept at Windsor, the public hearing of him only at monthly intervals when the principal newspapers published his doctors' bulletin of a couple of lines, which read—'His Majesty's bodily health is good, but his disorder continues undiminished.'—or a different arrangement of words conveying an identical message.

His son, the Prince Regent, was troubled also, unable to give his full attention to the history that was being made hour by hour. A daily coming and going of notes and messengers between Carlton House, his official residence, and Warwick House, the home of his daughter Charlotte, kept family tempers inflamed. Princess Charlotte was questioning the contract for her marriage to the Prince of Orange, with whom, in the beginning, she had been moderately taken. She was anxious not to be sent out of the country, partly because she did not want to abandon her mother, the Princess of Wales, who was at the height of her long quarrel with the Prince. Ellis Cornelia Knight, the Princess's tall waiting woman, was condemned to carry most of these letters and was a daily witness to explosions of Hanoverian rage. Miss Knight barely had leisure to notice the celebrations in the streets travelled by her carriage.

Rejoicings were also tempered, that first week, by anxiety for British soldiers in the field. Even while the bust of 'victorious Wellington' was being hoisted above the great transparency on Blades' Glass Works, reports were coming in that he was still fighting Marshal Soult near Toulouse, not having heard of Napoleon's fall. Soult was driven off towards Carcassonne. On entering Toulouse, Wellington found himself cheered in the streets, and a messenger from Bordeaux came in within the hour telling that the Emperor had abdicated. 'You don't say so, upon my honour! Hurrah!' cried Lord Wellington, 'spinning round and snapping his fingers.'[5]

Public discontent had mostly been forgotten in relief and jubilation at the peace. The principal grievance with the public in the spring of 1814 was the price of bread, which had risen in London to elevenpence for a quartern loaf. Now everybody hoped renewed trade with Europe would bring a quick reduction in prices. On the third day of the illuminations a new transparency appeared in the window of a cookshop in Fleet Street which drew the crowds away even from the nearby tree with its hissing gaslight blossoms. The picture showed 'John Bull seated at a table, with a captivating slice of roast beef on his plate, a bottle of brandy in the centre, a huge plum pudding above, and at the extremity a large loaf, with 7d. marked upon it'. The caption read 'John Bull himself again'.[1]

News had been coming in daily from Paris, telling of the rapture with which its people had received their conquerors.

The entry of the Allies into Paris, March 1814.

Louis XVIII landing at Calais, April 24th, 1814.

The Emperor of Russia, so moderate and magnanimous in his peace terms, was the hero of the day. One of his first public actions had been to go to a play. The Théâtre Français had hung up a new drop curtain in honour of his presence decorated with a crown and golden fleurs de lys. All over the city workmen were hastily effacing the Napoleonic emblems —the eagle, the bee, the capital letter N—and replacing them with lilies. French state prisoners had been released; children conscripted for state education against their parents' wishes were being sent home; priests who had refused to pray for Napoleon were given their liberty. Te Deums had been sung. On the arrival of 'Monsieur', Louis' brother, crowds turned out to escort him to the Tuileries, where he was the first person of royal blood to set foot for twenty-two years. The Emperor of Russia and the King of Prussia tactfully kept away from this demonstration, thinking it proper that his welcome should be entirely French. Lord Castlereagh thought it fitting that England, so long the home of the Bourbons, should be represented, and the entire British mission met 'Monsieur' at the city gates. That night they went with him to the Théâtre Français where 'The Hunting Party of Henry IV', a play banned under Napoleon's regime, was triumphantly revived. The performance was stopped a dozen times while the audience cheered royalist allusions and joined in popular songs. These rapturous demonstrations provoked as much delight in England as in France, though some people reacted differently. Wellington's attractive niece, Lady Burghersh wrote, 'what I own disgusted me was to see Monsieur surrounded by Talleyrand, Ney, Marmont, Oudinot, etc, the National Guard and the very populace who three weeks ago were shouting Vive l'Empereur!'[6] Lady Burghersh managed to be the first British civilian to reach Paris after the end of hostilities, travelling from Dijon in a carriage with only her personal servants, much to the chagrin of Castlereagh and other English gentlemen who had not thought it prudent to venture on the roads of France so soon.

Napoleon had been at the Palace of Fontainebleau since the surrender of Paris. Reports coming in about him during the first weeks of the peace were wildly contradictory. One day he was reported on his way to Elba; the next, he had not moved and was confined to the house by illness; he was raving mad; he had made an attempt on his own life; he was perfectly sane, indeed cheerful, and was making plans for his little new kingdom, asking for a botanist, a chemist and an astronomer to take to the island; he was planning to write his memoirs. When at last he was definitely reported gone, under escort of four commissioners of the Allied Powers, the tales of his leavetaking were equally confused. He had abandoned his faithful guards callously, with hardly a backward look; he had broken down and embraced them in a scene of affecting tears. When the papers had exhausted their stock of epithets on the fallen Emperor they turned their jibes on the rest of the Bonaparte family. 'Joseph will retain his Spanish cloak and Jerome his German small-clothes, and with these and some other odd title, such as the Knight of the Sorrowful Countenance and Baron Münchausen, they will go on their travels, it is said, where many worthy gentlemen have gone before them, "To the plantations in America".'[1]

France and England were alike bewildered at events which seemed to have altered the whole aspect of the civilised world. 'That Buonaparte, the Emperor of the French—the Protector of that vast fabrick the Confederation of the Rhine—the Mediator of Switzerland—the King of the finest portion of Italy—the creator of Nine Kingdoms, each acknowledged by the general consent of Europe—a Captain (till lately) of undisputed pre-eminence—who spread the devastation of his victories to a greater extent over Europe than any preceding Conqueror had ever done;—that this man, whom not a month ago France would have acknowledged as her Chief, and whose government Europe would have recognised as legitimate, should sink at once, with no "gradation of decay" into absolute insignificance and obscurity,—yet secure in his person, and unmolested in his person,—is an event that we believe to be unparalleled in the annals of human creation.'[2]

The uncrowned king of France, Louis le Desiré, as everybody now remembered he had been called, delayed his return to French soil because of a particularly severe attack of gout. In spite of the state of his legs and feet, on which he could not tolerate leather, wearing instead a pair of clumsy velvet boots, and his enormous pear-shaped body, he was a not unattractive man. His complexion was pink and healthy, his large eyes lustrous. He had an engaging manner and a gift for making spontaneous compliments that won the hearts of the most prejudiced hearers. On Wednesday, April 20th, the day Napoleon was escorted from Fontainebleau on his way to exile, Louis was brought to London on the first stage of his triumphant journey home, and London's citizens, who had calmed down somewhat after the illuminations of the previous week, all turned out to watch his arrival. Grillon's Hotel in Albemarle Street, had been prepared as his temporary palace. The rooms he was to occupy were hung, by order of the Prince Regent, with crimson velvet embroidered with golden fleurs de lys.

The village of Stanmore was decked with flowers and ribbons and there was hardly a cloud in the sky when the Prince Regent arrived at the Abercorn Arms to meet his royal guest. The men of Stanmore rode out to Hartwell, where they dismounted, unhitched the horses from Louis' carriage, and, on foot, dragged the King in triumph to the village, where the Prince was waiting on the inn doorstep to

embrace him in French fashion. Louis was dressed in black
and gold, the Prince in uniform with Russian and English
orders. At Kilburn Wells their procession was joined by a
squad of Horse Guards, who conducted them into London
by way of Cumberland Gate. All the way to Piccadilly the
balconies were hung with ribbons and white flowers. The
parks were packed solid with 'a mass of carriages, females of
the first fashion standing on the seats.'² Miss Berry ventured
out to watch Louis' entry, but was frustrated by the dense-
ness of the crowd. All she managed to see was seven of the
Prince's carriages, each drawn by six horses, and preceded
by several hundred gentlemen on horseback. 'The people,'
she noted in her diary, 'took off their hats and saluted the
carriages as they passed with much good will, but without
the least enthusiasm.'³ Their sympathies, at this moment, lay
rather with the Princess than the Prince of Wales.

The day had started badly for their daughter, the Princess
Charlotte, with a morning call from her uncle the Duke of
York and a Mr Adam. Her letters protesting at her marriage
contract struck Adam as being far too erudite to have been
composed by a mere female and he wondered who her 'legal
adviser' could be. Miss Knight reminded him that Charlotte
had had a legal training, but he only smiled in a disbelieving
way. The visit left Charlotte hurt and agitated. Her next
caller, the Grand Duchess of Oldenburg, helped to restore
her good humour. The Princess liked and was flattered by
the attentions paid her by this striking Russian lady, sister of
Europe's present hero, the Emperor Alexander. The Duchess
had been in London for three weeks and had made a sensa-
tion by her energy, her eagerness to meet everybody and see
every sight, from historical monuments to the inner work-
ings of Mr Whitbread's brewery. She was a widow, and had
recently been spoken of as a possible future wife for the
Regent if he were ever able to free himself from Princess

Caroline. At the moment, however, the Prince did not look on her with favour, rightly suspecting that she was helping to stiffen Charlotte's opposition to the disputed marriage contract. He had instructed Miss Knight to do all she could to prevent his daughter seeing much of the Grand Duchess, but Miss Knight protested it was not her place to prevent the royal lady calling at Warwick House if she had a mind to.

The Grand Duchess of Oldenburg was living in the Pulteney Hotel, which overlooked the route of Louis' procession. She had, perhaps, a little exceeded her position as an honoured royal visitor by inviting the Queen of England to come to her rooms to get a good view. The Queen had politely declined, but did not prevent her daughters, the Princesses Elizabeth and Mary, from accepting. The Grand Duchess served breakfast to a large gathering of distinguished ladies when they came in from her balcony after watching Louis pass. To them was added, at the last moment, Princess Charlotte and Miss Knight, who had gone out to the park with the intention of watching the procession, but, like Miss Berry, had eventually despaired of making their way through the crowd. Finding themselves near the doors of Pulteney's, they had ventured to ask for the Grand Duchess and were received in a very civil manner. The Tzar's sister took a good deal of pleasure in stirring up trouble and was delighted to welcome the Princess precisely because she knew the Regent would be annoyed. The Prince's sisters, Mary and Elizabeth, received their niece coldly and the occasion turned out to be no pleasure to poor Charlotte. On the way home her carriage was held up by affectionate demonstrations from the public, who took every opportunity of showing its displeasure with the Regent by acclaiming his wife and daughter. 'Wherever Princess Charlotte appeared this was now the case,' wrote Miss Knight, 'though she by no means sought it.'[7]

Miss Knight had been presented to the Tzar's sister on the
1st April, the day after she had arrived in England, when
there had been a party in her honour at Carlton House. Here
the Grand Duchess had caused the first of many scenes she
was to make in London by leaving the room abruptly the
moment the Prince's orchestra struck up. Music had a
disastrous effect on her nerves and her violent reaction made
it almost impossible for any to be played at royal functions in
the spring of that year. She was also said to be subject to
fainting fits and hardly to have slept since the death of her
husband. Her nerves had been ruined at the time of the
burning of Moscow. Miss Knight described her to her diary.
'Her figure was slight and well-formed, her complexion
good, her eyes fine, and her manners dignified, called grace-
ful, but I think not gracefully feminine, at least not when
she spoke, her nose real Calmuck, and, altogether, I thought
her very like what I remembered of her father, only I liked
his manners better.'[7]

That night Louis went to bed exhausted. The day had
been full of comings and goings by the French royal family
in exile; the old Prince de Condé and the young Duc de
Bourbon, and the romantic, if rather plain and glum,
Duchesse d'Angoulême, who was doubly his niece, being the
daughter of his brother, Louis XVI, and the wife of his
nephew, son of 'Monsieur', the Comte d'Artois. Before he
could leave for France Louis had to face two days of receptions, of being gazed at, bowed to and shaken by the hand
by anybody and everybody bold enough to effect an entrance
to Grillon's Hotel. Thursday was reserved for the highly
placed, who called in full court dress—the royal dukes, the
cabinet ministers and foreign ambassadors, the officers of the
royal households, whose carriages were so numerous that
the streets were again impassable round Piccadilly and the
palaces. Friday was free-for-all, when 'entré was granted to

any person who chose to enter, and but few left with dry
eyes.'[8] On Thursday Louis dined at Carlton House with the
Regent and the Archbishop of Canterbury. It was at this
party that Prinny conferred on him the Order of the Garter,
remarking afterwards that clasping it round that gouty knee
had felt like putting a girdle round the waist of a stoutish
woman.

Fanny d'Arblay, still prostrated by the death of her father,
Dr Burney, had no thought of joining in the loyal demonstrations until she received a letter from Windsor Castle that
could not be ignored. It desired her to take the necessary
steps to get herself presented to 'Son Altesse Royale Madame
la Duchesse d'Angoulême, who was to have a drawing-room
in London, both for French and English, on the day preceding her departure for France. The letter added that I must
waive all objections relative to my recent loss, as it would be
improper, in the present state of things, that the wife of a
general officer should not be presented.' Accordingly she
put herself in the hands of Lady Crewe, who undertook to
organize the meeting and booked a room at Grillon's where
they could wait in comfort and privacy, Monsieur Grillon
having 'once been cook to her lord.' Fanny went with a
heavy heart, determined to keep decently in the background
and expecting to take little pleasure in the experience, but it
was not long before her novelist's eye began to be diverted by
other arrivals, beginning with an 'uncommon trio—a
gentleman, middle-aged, of a most pleasing appearance and
address, . . . accompanied by a young man with a sensible
look; and a young lady, pretty, gentle, and engaging, with
languishing soft eyes, though with a smile and an expression
of countenance that showed an innate disposition to archness
and sport.' These attractive people were introduced as 'the
celebrated Irish orator, Mr Grattan, and his son and daughter.' Fanny had soon forgotten her mourning. 'The crowd,

... for they deserve a better name than mob, interested my observation still more. John Bull has seldom appeared to me to greater advantage. I never saw him *en masse* behave with such impulsive propriety. Enchanted to behold a King of France in his capital; conscious that *le grand Monarque* was fully in his power; yet honestly enraptured to see that "the King would enjoy his own again", and enjoy it through the generous efforts of his rival, brave, noble old England; he yet seemed aware that it was fitting to subdue all exuberance of pleasure, which, else, might annoy, if not alarm, his royal guest. He took care, therefore, that his delight should not amount to exultation; it was quiet and placid, though pleased and curious; I had almost said it was gentleman-like.'⁹

It now turned out, to Fanny's acute embarrassment, that Lady Crewe had brought her to the wrong place. Though Louis VIII was in residence, the Duchesse d'Angoulême was not present, nor was she expected. They should have gone to the house in South Audley Street where 'Monsieur' had his London residence. Fanny was aghast, the more so because Lady Crewe now determined not to leave Grillon's without seeing her protégé, since she was on the spot, shaking the hand of the King himself.

After a good deal of manoeuvring on Lady Crewe's part and attempts to get lost in the background on Fanny's they found themselves in the audience chamber. Louis came in and 'took his seat, with an air of mingled sweetness and dignity... The Duc de Duras stood at his left hand, and was the Grand Maître des Cérémonies... The presentations were short, and without much mark or likelihood. The men bowed low and passed on; the ladies curtseyed and did the same. Those who were not known gave a card, I think, to the Duc de Duras; who named them; those of former acquaintance with his Majesty simply made their obeisance.'

There were a great many French people and Fanny noted that the Duc, out of anxiety not to tire his King, hurried them past in a manner that bordered on rudeness—'yet the English, by express command of His Majesty, had always the preference and always took place of the French; which was an attention of the King in return for the asylum he had here found, that he seemed to delight to display... When it came to the turn of Lady Crewe, who, being known to the King, was not named, she declined to be hustled on by the Duc, stopping beside him and saying in a loud whisper, "Voilà Madame d'Arblay; il faut qu'elle soit presentée".'[9]

Fanny now found herself 'hot and cold and cold and hot, alternately, with excess of embarrassment', but the Duc de Duras recognized her and she saw that escape was out of the question. But when the dreaded moment came and the Duc seized her hand and drew her towards the King's chair, a sudden singular change came over her and she found herself 'all courage and animation'. 'When his Majesty took my hand,' she wrote, '—or rather, took hold of my fist—and said, in very pretty English: "I am very happy to see you," I felt such a glow of satisfaction, that, involuntarily, I burst forth with its expression, incoherently, but delightedly and irresistibly, though I cannot remember how. He certainly was not displeased, for his smile was brightened and his manner was most flattering, as he repeated that he was very glad to see me, and added that he had known me; "though without sight, very long: for I have *read* you—and been charmed with your books—charmed and entertained. I have read them very often, I know them very well indeed; and I have long wanted to know *you*!"... When he stopped, and let go my hand, I curtsied respectfully, and was moving on; but he again caught my *fist*, and, fixing me, with looks of strong though smiling investigation, he appeared archly desirous to read the lines of my face, as if to deduce from them the qualities of my mind. His manner, however, was so polite and so gentle that he did not at all discountenance me; and though he resumed the praise of my little works, he uttered the panegyric with a benignity so gay as well as flattering, that I felt enlivened, nay, elevated, with a joy that overcame *mauvaise honte.*'⁹

The Duc de Duras now put in a word for the absent Monsieur d'Arblay, perhaps thinking that Fanny, with this praise of her *Evelina*, her *Cecilia* and *Camilla*, was getting too much of the limelight. 'Et Monsieur d'Arblay, Sire, .. est un des plus devoués et fidèles serviteurs de votre Majesté,' he said. 'Je le crois'⁹ said the King, seizing Fanny for the third time by the fist.

The Duchesse d'Angoulême's reception at South Audley Street was somewhat depleted. Fanny never got there, and Lady Shelley did not have time, either, lingering too long at Albemarle Street listening to cries of 'Vive le Roi', enchanted with the King's dignity of manner. Lady Shelley managed to catch sight of the Duchesse at a royal reception before the end of the day and declared that she had 'grown quite pretty since the change in their fortunes. "Le bonheur embellit tout".'⁸

At eight the next morning, Saturday, April 23rd, Louis set out from Albemarle Street, cheered by a fresh crowd. 'God bless your Majesty! A happy return to your native land!'¹ The Prince Regent had gone ahead to Dover to receive him. The Duke of Sussex escorted his carriage over the Thames and to the borders of Kent, where it was handed over to the Lord Lieutenant of the county and a party of Volunteer Cavalry. Before setting out, Louis made an impromptu speech, thanking the Regent and the people of England for all they had done for him in his exile and giving them the entire credit for his happy restoration. This heartfelt but informal utterance was heard by reporters from the principal

London papers who unfortunately printed it verbatim. The speech was read and discussed abroad and became the innocent cause of much coldness between the Allied Sovereigns. As Louis departed Miss Berry did some arithmetic for her diary. 'If about the same interval elapses between the visits of the Kings of France to London, we shall not see another for five hundred years.'³

All the way through Kent the roads were lined with spectators; bells rang from village churches; wherever cannon were to be found they were shot off at Louis' approach. Canterbury, Gravesend and Chatham were *en fête*. One unfortunate incident only marred the glorious procession. At Sittingbourne, the Parish Clerk, overcome with an excess of patriotic fervour, approached too near the wheels of the royal carriage and was run over. He died the following Wednesday.

That evening the King and the Regent dined aboard the frigate *Jason*. They returned to sleep on land, Louis in state apartments in the castle, Prinny in a room in the principal bank. The port of Dover was lit up, not with elaborate gaslights and transparencies, but by hundreds of common candles, expressing the people's congratulations 'more intelligibly than the finest decorations which are on such occasions so lavishly scattered through the proud metropolis'.¹ Every window of every house was alight from top to bottom; everybody wore the white cockade; every Frenchman was an honoured visitor. Across the Channel Lord Castlereagh was signing the Convention for the Cessation of Hostilities; all war was to cease by sea and land; the blockade was to be raised, prisoners were to be returned without exchange or ransom.

Next morning, while the Prince Regent stood waving on the furthest point of the harbour pier, the yacht *Royal Sovereign*, with the Bourbon family on board, set sail for

Calais in bright sunlight and a favourable breeze. The entire fleet, under the command of the Duke of Clarence, passed by in mid-Channel to salute the royal yacht, which was seen to enter the Calais roadstead at about 3 p.m. The Regent drove back in the warm spring afternoon to a London that was relaxing after a fortnight of high living.

That night Prinny's unhappy wife gave a dinner at Kensington Palace—'well-composed and tolerably agreeable.'[3] The Irish orator, Mr Grattan, was invited, with his attractive daughter, and Lady Crewe was there. Her friend, Madame d'Arblay, had returned to the obscurity of family mourning. Also at the Princess's table Mary Berry noted Lord and Lady Claremont, Lord Leveson-Gower, Lord Barrington, Mr Canning, Lord Byron and Mr Plunkett. She also noticed that 'the Princess has not the same cheerfulness to excite others as she had at one time.'[3]

CHAPTER II

The Bourbons Return to Paris

THE Convention for the Suppression of Hostilities, signed by Castlereagh on the 23rd, had been anticipated. Prisoners had already come back from France and the blockade had not been operating for a fortnight. On the day that Louis came to London from Stanmore gay parties had set out from Dover for a day's sight-seeing on the other side of the Channel. A number of English ladies spent the day in Calais, where they were delighted at being received 'with marked respect', the inhabitants crying out 'Vivent les Anglais! Vive Louis XVIII! Vivent les Bourbons!'[1] as they disembarked on the quay, and asking anxiously, 'Will our king ever come?'[2] The ladies partook of a meal at Dessein's, the enormous hotel, eating in a room which, they were told, had lately been occupied by the ci-devant Empress. The people in the streets were cheerful and friendly, though their clothes were ragged and their shoes old. The town showed every sign of the privations of war; the houses dilapidated and in need of paint, the shops empty of luxuries. The high proportion of women caused much comment. Conscription had removed so many of the menfolk that even the apothecaries' shops were staffed entirely by females. People were busy effacing Napoleonic emblems from the buildings in preparation for Louis' arrival, but the visitors detected a lurking admiration for the late Emperor in the conversation

of some of Calais' inhabitants. They were relieved to be rid
of the trouble he had caused them, but still cherished the
memory of his military glory.

Napoleon's memory was temporarily obliterated on the
25th when the *Royal Sovereign* was sighted offshore. For
hours before she docked the quays were lined with citizens
'of the most respectable appearance',[2] everybody having
ransacked their wardrobes for their best and least worn
clothes. Every lady who possessed a white dress had put it on
regardless of fashion. The boats in the harbour ran up flags,
sand was strewn over the streets and patterns made on it
with branches of leaves and spring flowers, the balconies
were hung with garlands and tapestries. The town looked
as if it had been decked for one of the Corpus Christi processions banned since the Revolution. When he had set his foot
once more on French soil, Louis was put in a carriage and
drawn, as at Stanmore, by a concourse of young men. The
Duchesse d'Angoulême was welcomed by a bevy of girls in
white. 'After more than twenty years of absence, Heaven
gives my children back to me, Heaven gives me back to my
children; come, let us thank God in his Temple,'[2] said
Louis. Mass was said by a curé who had been exiled for
having refused to swear the oath to Napoleon. The Royal
Family went to Dessein's to rest before dining in public.
The places of honour at Louis' table were filled by English
people, Lord Sidmouth, the Earl of Buckingham, Lord
Cawdor and Lord William Fitzroy. After the meal Louis
paid 'particular attention to the English women'[1] and
M. Pigault Maubaillereq and the ladies of the town joined
in a new anthem, sung to the tune of God Save the King.

> *'Grand Dieu! Sauve le Roi,*
> *Notre espoir est en toi,*
> *Sauve le Roi.*

Qu'il soit toujours heureux,
Puissant et glorieux,
C'est l'objet de nos voeux,
Sauve le Roi.'[3]

The King and his suite set out for Paris next morning, making a slow journey that lasted a week. Louis slept at Boulogne, Abbeville, Amiens, Compiègne, and his castle of St Ouen, three miles outside the capital.

The place on the pier at Calais where the King had descended from the *Royal Sovereign* had been carefully marked in chalk. The moment he left the town a stone-mason was set to work to chip out an imprint of the gouty royal foot as a permanent memorial of the Restoration. This footprint, pointed out by douaniers to the flood of passengers from across the sea, became, for a month or two, the object of passionate veneration, and many an Englishman was surprised and embarrassed to see his travelling companions, the returning émigrés and exiles, flinging themselves on their knees to embrace it with happy tears.

'Our passage to Calais was rendered very interesting,' wrote Sir Archibald Alison, who crossed with his friend Patrick Frazer-Tytler in the first week of May, 'by the number of Frenchmen who accompanied us. Some of these were emigrants, who had spent the best part of their lives in exile; the greater part were prisoners of various ranks, who had been taken at different periods of the war. There was evidently the greatest diversity of character, of prospects, of previous habits, and of political and moral sentiments among these men; the only bond that connected them was the love of their common country; and at a moment for which they had been so long and anxiously looking, this was sufficient to repress all jealousy and discord, and to unite them cordially and sincerely in the sentiment which was expressed,

with true French enthusiasm, by one of the party, as we left
the harbour of Dover,—"Voilà notre chère France,—à
present nous sommes tous amis!"'[4]

This ill-assorted collection of royalists and soldiers of
Bonaparte, of exiled priests and disciples of Liberté,
Egalité, Fraternité, continued to entertain the two Scotsmen
all the way over the Channel. 'The expressions of their
emotions in words, looks and gestures, was sometimes
extremely pleasing, at other times irresistibly ludicrous, but
always characteristic of a people whose natural feelings are
quick and lively, and who have no idea of there being any
dignity or manliness in repressing or concealing them. When
the boat approached the shore, a fine young officer, who had
been one of the most amusing of our companions, leapt from
the prow, and taking up a handful of sand, kissed it with an
expression of ardent feeling and enthusiastic joy, which it
was delightful to observe.'[4]

Sir Archibald and Mr Frazer-Tytler, a pair of Edinburgh
law students, had left their city still almost in the grip of
winter and had been enchanted by their journey through
the smiling spring-time of Kent. 'The extent and excellence
of the cultivation; the thriving condition of the towns, and
the smiling aspect of the neat and clean villages through
which we passed; the luxuriant bloom of the fruit trees
surrounding them; the number of beautiful villas adapted to
the accommodation of the middle rank of society, the crowds
of well-dressed peasantry going to or returning from church;
the frank and cheerful countenance of the men, and the
beauty of the women—all presented a most pleasing
spectacle.'[4] The contrast between their own country and
Southern England had been striking. In France they were
reminded again of Scotland. 'All the lower ranks of the
people, besides being much worse-looking than the English,
were much more coarsely clothed, and they seemed utterly

indifferent about the appearance of their dress. Very few of the men wore beaver hats, and hardly two had exactly the same kind of covering for their heads... The lower people appeared to bear a much stronger resemblance to some of the Highland clans, and to the Welsh, than to any other inhabitants of Britain. They were struck, like British travellers before and since, by the lack of hedges and enclosures, which gave, to people used to the neat chequer-board fields of England, a bare and wild appearance to the landscape. Many of the fields had been left unplanted, with 'a few sheep and long-legged lean hogs' turned out on them 'to pick up a miserable subsistence.'[4]

The vagaries of the wind and tide had landed Alison and Tytler three miles along the coast from Calais, so they had a long walk in which to observe these details. They did not escape the attention of the douaniers, and their supporting rabble of soldiery who 'seemed rather the fragments of broken up gangs, than the remains of a force that had been steady and controlled, and lawful. They have ... much expression of intelligence, and often of ferocity in their countenance, .. there are few of them who an Englishman, judging from his recollections of English soldiers, would recognize to belong to an army.'[4]

Arrived at Calais, the Scotsmen found themselves hailed with much pleasure by the citizens, with cries of 'Vivent les Anglais' and 'Vive le Roi'. Perhaps because of their nationality, they were quick to detect 'interested motives' in the general joy expressed, motives that the lady visitors of the previous week had missed. 'A number of blackguard-looking men gathered round us, recommending their own services, and different hotels, with much vehemence, and violent altercations among themselves; and troops of children followed, crying "Vivent les Anglais—Give me one sou".'[4]

The packet boats continued to arrive, four or five a day,

every one bringing twice as many passengers as their permitted load. The hotels and lodging houses were filled to bursting, the Diligences being too few to take all the arrivals on the second stage of their journey. Sir Archibald found them booked for ten days ahead, so he and his companion went to visit a *maison des chaises* which reminded them of 'The Sentimental Journey' and contrived to hire a private carriage. They set out the next day accompanied by a French officer who had been a prisoner in Scotland and who had given them much kindness and attention on the crossing. The inns on the way to the capital had seen better days, being imposing and large, but unpainted and full of battered old furniture. The horses in the carriages were harnessed with rope. 'There were few carts, and hardly any four-wheeled carriages to be seen in the streets; and it was obvious that the internal communications in this part of the country were very limited.'[4]

Such posting as there was was 'scrupulously attended to',[5] in theory, at any rate. Most travellers compared it favourably with arrangements in England. 'There is no competition on the road,' wrote Edward Planta in his new guide to Paris, 'those who arrive first are uniformly first accommodated: neither is any driver permitted to pass another on the road, unless the carriage which goes before breaks down, or the harness gives way. It may not be amiss to inform the reader that for a very trifling sum he may purchase the "Etat des Postes Généraux", a volume alphabetically arranged, containing all the posts throughout France, the precise distance of every place, and the sum to be paid both at the post houses and to the drivers; by this means it is impossible that he can be subject to the smallest imposition.'[8] The public Diligences were constructed to carry six persons, and the conductor in charge was responsible for the safety of his passengers and of their baggage.

The Paris towards which the Scottish travellers were heading was 'at the moment the most wonderful show-box in the world.'[5] The Honourable J. W. Ward described it in a letter to Mary Berry. 'It has within its walls as many live Emperors, Kings, generals and eminent persons of all kinds as the ingenious Mr Salmon ever presented in wax. . . I say nothing of princes and prime ministers, though they are here in plenty.'[5]

Louis might have been forgiven for believing that he had arrived in a foreign country, so many languages other than French were to be heard in the streets. '"Ukases" in the Russian tongue, addressed to the non-ruling part of the population . . . are everywhere stuck on the walls. One walks in safety about the streets of Paris, under the protection of Count Sacken, the governor of the place. You are stared at when you speak French at the gate of a French garrison town, and are obliged, if you can, to explain yourself in German. In this pleasant and honourable situation, the common people seem gay and self satisfied.'[5] On the roads between Calais and the capital French uniforms were decidedly in the minority. Everywhere the travellers saw great-coated Cossacks, stiff-shakoed Prussians, the red jackets of British troops making their way home towards the Channel, even a sprinkling of kilted Highlanders. With the exception of the Prussians, all these conquerors seemed on the best of terms with the conquered.

Ward had come to Paris, one of a flood of eager sight-seers, by the route the royal party was now taking. 'In every town or village through which I passed, I found the inhabitants collected; their houses were adorned with flowers and laurels, and everything seemed to indicate that they were awaiting the approach of some victorious French generals, or celebrating the anniversary of some great national triumph. I must observe, however, that though they received the foreign princes better than one could expect, they showed no great enthusiasm for the first appearance of their own sovereign.'[5]

Louis approached his capital calmly. His gout had not been improved by travel and excitement. If he felt the welcome accorded him by his own subjects fell short of the enthusiasm he had seen in London or Kent, he was careful not to show his disappointment. His situation was, after all, peculiar. The defeat of France's enemies would have been his ruin; their victory was his salvation. His Marshals, who came out along the route to greet him, had, only a fortnight before, been Bonaparte's Marshals, fighting the foreigners who were to set him on his throne. There was no lack of decorations, of services of thanksgiving in the churches along the way, of polite speeches. A sufficient number of young ladies in white turned out, at each stopping-place, to present bouquets to Marie Antoinette's daughter and to serenade her with the chorus Gluck had written for her mother. Her little English bonnet drew amused comment from the ladies of a nation where 'monstrous three-tiered headdresses' were the fashionable wear. Though constantly quoted as saying 'How happy I am to be in the midst of the good French people', she was equally often described to be in tears. Arrived at Compiègne, Louis played host to almost all the great and famous, who rode out from Paris to pay their respects. The Emperor Alexander arrived in a plain carriage without retinue, in a manner typical of his behaviour at this moment, and was closeted with him for some hours. 'Monsieur', his brother, and the Duc de Berri, his nephew, came out to complete the family party. The Marshals assembled in the audience chamber—Macdonald, Ney, Moncey, Serrurier, Mortier, Brune, Berthier, Lefebvre, Oudinot and Kellermann. Still in his monstrous red velvet gaiters, bound with gold ribbon, Louis rose unsteadily from his chair and held out his arms to the two nearest; 'It is on you, Marshals, I wish always to support myself; approach and surround me. You have always been good Frenchmen. I hope France will no longer have need of your swords. If ever, which God forbid, we are forced to draw them, afflicted as I am with gout, I will march with you.'¹ 'Sire,' replied the Marshals, 'be pleased to consider us the pillars of Your Majesty's throne. It is our wish to be its firmest support.'¹ After dinner, to the astonishment of the reporter on the *Journal des Débats*, the King invited his Marshals to sit with him in the drawing-room. 'These brave captains appeared singularly moved by this kindness on the part of the sovereign. They remembered that the foreigner (Napoleon) without regard to their age, their labours, and their wounds, had forced them to stand for hours in his presence, as if he measured the respect of his servants by the pains he made them endure.'²

The arrival of Talleyrand, on the next day, caused the greatest stir of interest. How would this man, with his inexpressive toad face and diamond eyes and his genius for being on the winning side, present himself? The onlookers expected him to be 'complaisant, adroit, flattering, and caressing; but he chose quite another role. He was cold and serious, and made advances to nobody, acting like a man who had nothing to accuse himself of and who stood in no need of support.'² Louis had every reason to distrust the man who had virtually been running Paris since its surrender, who had lent his own house to the Emperor of Russia, who, no doubt, he had firmly by the ear. He received him with an equal coldness, but politely, and many of the company present were delighted to see Talleyrand kept waiting for his audience three hours.

On May 2nd, while Louis rested at St Ouen, regulations were published for his formal entry into Paris—all flower-pots to be removed from window-sills; no carriages or hackney coaches permitted in the streets; nobody on foot or horse to cross the processional route; no one to climb on buildings or erect stages to watch from; there must be no squibs or firecrackers. *The Times* thought England might well profit from these ideas, but was glad her people did not have to be warned, as the French were, not to deposit rubbish or filth.

The great day dawned calm and cloudless, 'never did a finer day give light to a finer spectacle', a circumstance which must have lightened the heart of Madame Blanchard, the intrepid aeronaut, who planned to celebrate the occasion by ascending in her balloon the moment Louis entered the Porte St Denis, releasing a flight of doves over the city. Nobody went to work, but everyone was up early, wreathing their balconies with the usual white flowers and garlands and hanging curtains and tablecloths out of their windows. By order of the Allied Sovereigns foreign uniforms vanished from the streets. The Sovereigns themselves, the Emperors of Austria and Russia and the King of Prussia, inconspicuously dressed, sat watching at the windows of a private house, taking care not to be recognised. Among an escort of fourteen carriages King Louis XVIII entered his city by the decorated Porte St Denis, riding in an open landau drawn by eight white horses, a present from the Prince Regent which he had brought with him from Dover. He wore the blue coat and epaulettes of a general and was observed to be weeping. On his left the Duchesse d'Angoulême, in white with a veil and feathers on her head, looked 'tender and melancholy'. Bells pealed, and artillery, 'which henceforth will announce only festivals of peace',[1] was heard all over the city. There was only one anxious moment, when Mme Blanchard's balloon, instead of ascending straight upwards, 'reclined for an instant on the statue of Henri IV'.[1] She freed it with a pull on a rope and sailed away over the Palace of the Four Nations, scattering her emblems of peace as she went.

Louis' first official action was to hear Te Deum at Notre Dame, into which Talleyrand had the effrontery to conduct him, re-assuming the manner of his discarded priesthood. The joy of the occasion was marred for royalists by the knowledge that 'certain regicides of the Convention'[2] were in the vast congregation. The Duc de Vitrolles had pleaded with Pasquier, Chief of Police, to have them excluded, but it was useless. It was no wonder to him that the Duchesse looked 'pale, trembling, and weak to the point of swooning.'[2] She actually did swoon when she reached the steps of the Tuileries, though whether from exhaustion, from the strain of having to pass by her mother's last prison, or from the shock of being received at the palace door by a hundred and forty-four ladies (twelve for each district of France) in snowy white, is not certain.

The London papers' accounts of the reception suggest it was unclouded. 'The whole population assembled to witness the joyous entré;.. their enthusiasm was boundless.'[6] 'The National Guard seemed to wait with impatience the noblest reward of their exertions—that of receiving the descendant of Henry IV.'[1] Eyewitnesses among the visitors were not so certain of the public temper. Mr Ward, who watched from a place near the city gate, wrote his doubts to Miss Berry. 'The ceremony was as magnificent as possible, and the crowds, of course, prodigious; but I thought the applause feeble for the occasion. They cried "Vive le Roi" from a recollection that, under these circumstances, it would be wrong to omit it. In short, the applause resembled a little that which, at private theatricals, is, by the well-bred part of the company, bestowed on the lady of the house. The fact, I believe, is that the people have become quite callous by what they have suffered for the last twenty years, and that no

public event makes much impression on them. They are
generally well inclined to the Bourbons, not, however, as a
positive good, but as the least of the evils they are likely to
endure.'⁵ Some of the French, too, confided their doubts to
their diaries, noting that the soldiers of the National Guard
seemed hostile, as if lamenting Napoleon. 'On the day of the
entry of the King,' wrote Bourrienne, 'there was no such
enthusiasm as on that when "Monsieur", the King's brother,
came to Paris.'²

If the population was only tepidly polite in its reception of
the restored monarch, it was extraordinarily warm in the
'shouts and vivas'² it bestowed on the three conquerors.
When the Royal Family was safely installed in the Tuileries,
the Allied Sovereigns came out of hiding and the occupying
troops were let loose from their camps in the Bois de
Boulogne. The Tzar Alexander, with his benevolent moon
face, his hat with the sweeping plumes and the uniform that
disguised the deficiencies of his figure—nipped-in waist and
extravagantly padded shoulders under large epaulettes—was
the principal object of public adulation. His modesty won
him golden opinions. When the statue of Napoleon had
been taken down from the vast brass-coated column he had
erected in the Place Vendôme, a deputation of Parisians
waited on the Emperor to beg him to allow his own to be put
in its place. 'His answer was, . . that it was too high for him
to mount; he should be afraid of falling down.'¹ He was
generally seen in company with Frederick-William, the
glum King of Prussia who had hardly been seen to smile
since the untimely death of his beautiful wife. They went
together, almost nightly, to opera or theatre, arm in arm,
dressed in unadorned uniform and without a single attendant. Their appearance in a box, generally when the
performance was well started, would stop the play. Audience
and actors joined in cheering them and in singing patriotic

songs. In contrast, the thin, pale, long-faced Francis of Austria went everywhere in the greatest possible state. As the father of Marie-Louise, Napoleon's wife, his position was equivocal and he trod warily. One day, however, he saw a portrait of his daughter in the Palace of the Legislative Body and tentatively offered to buy it. He was greatly moved and reassured at having his offer firmly rejected. The Princess 'had merited, in so many respects, the gratitude and veneration of the French, that the Legislative Body could not part with it.'[1]

On the day after his entry, Louis reclined comfortably in an armchair at the window of his palace to see the grand parade of Allied troops. The three sovereigns, making their first formal call, stood round him, Alexander explaining the spectacle. As the great procession passed, three men in civilian dress rode up and sat watching on the far side of it, Sir Charles Stewart, the British Ambassador, his half brother, Lord Castlereagh, and, between them, a hook-nosed man in a blue frock coat and top hat. The monarchs craned forward to get a sight of the newcomer. Lord Wellington had arrived that afternoon from the army at Toulouse. They saw Stewart introduce him to old Platoff the Cossack general. When Wellington saw the Russian cavalry he said 'in his plain way, "Well, to be sure, we can't turn out anything like this."'[7]

That night at a ball for four hundred people at Sir Charles Stewart's, Wellington was brought face to face with old General Blücher. The two men bowed, and 'looked at one another for five minutes before they spoke a word.'[2] Before the ball, the British commander had a private call from Alexander, who had rushed round to his lodgings the moment he left the Tuileries. Wellington stayed at the Ambassador's till six the next morning, watching Alexander dance with Maréchale Ney, Lady Castlereagh and the ambassadorial wives, but it was he who was the centre of attraction, and at one point the dancing was made impossible by the queue of persons that had formed up for the honour of shaking his hand.

That night, while the Allied conquerors danced in Paris, the exiled Bonaparte was spending his first evening in his new kingdom of Elba, having been conducted there on an English frigate by officers of the Russian, Austrian and British staff. The island saluted its new ruler with 101 guns and the mayor gave a reception for him at Porto Ferraio. The people appeared to receive the fallen emperor with cheerfulness, but this may have been short lived. Not long afterwards it was reported that, as his first official action, the new ruler had doubled their taxes.

In Paris, news was brought to Wellington that he had been promoted to a Dukedom. Ward met him at Lord Aberdeen's headquarters and wrote to Miss Berry. 'He seems quite unspoilt by success. He has not even contracted that habit of silence and reserve which so often accompanies dignity and favour... He is just as gay, frank and ready to converse.'[5] Someone mentioned that they believed he had never met Bonaparte in person and the Duke replied, 'I would at any time rather have heard a reinforcement of 40,000 men had joined the French army, than that he had arrived to take command.' Ward remarked, 'I had heard the opinion ascribed to him before, but I was glad to find he had the liberality to repeat it after Bonaparte's fall.'[5]

Sir Archibald Alison and Patrick Frazer-Tytler had arrived in the capital in their hired carriage in time to take seats for the Opera on the occasion Wellington made his first appearance there. 'He was received with loud applause, and the modesty of his demeanour, while it accorded with the impression of his character derived from his whole conduct, and the style of his public writings, sufficiently showed,

that his time had been spent more in camps than in courts.'
In the streets they heard Russian and Prussian officers saying,
'He is the hero of the war;—we have conquered the French
by main force, but his triumphs are the result of superior
skill.'[4]

The two students found Paris a place of balls and fêtes.
The weather had continued sparkling since the surrender,
dry, sunny and warm for the time of year. There were
military reviews in the parks, alfresco concerts, orchestras
playing in the public gardens. The theatres were doing
astonishing business, packed every night with foreigners and
with French people curious to stare at the great and famous.
There was only one blot on the managers' satisfaction. None
of them had so far received a visit from the Royal Family.
Before he could decently attend any place of entertainment,
Louis had to perform a pious duty to his murdered pre-
decessors. Accordingly Notre Dame, so recently the scene of
rejoicings, was hung with black to exclude all daylight, and,
on May 16th, lit only by hundreds of wax tapers, High Mass
was performed for the souls of Louis XVI, Marie Antoinette
and the Dauphin. It was not yet known where the actual
bodies had been buried, and the coffins, placed among the
tapers in the centre of the choir, were only symbolical. The
crowd that followed Louis into the church was larger than
at the rejoicings and many people failed to get tickets. Once
again there were complaints that among the so-called
mourners were people who were in part responsible for the
murder of those they were pretending to mourn, but the
'greater part', thought Alison, 'exhibited symptoms of
genuine sorrow, and seemed to participate in the solemnity
with unfeigned devotion.'[4] The Scotsmen, unused to
Catholic ceremony, were somewhat repelled by the vast
number of prelates assembled and the elaboration of the
worship, but they could not help being impressed. 'All that

art could devise was exhausted to render the scene impressive in the eyes of the people. To us, however, who had been habituated to the simplicity of the English form, the variety of unmeaning ceremony, the endless gestures and unceasing bows of the clergy who officiated, destroyed the impression which the solemnity of the service would otherwise have produced. But though the service itself appeared ridiculous, the effect of the whole scene was sublime in the greatest degree. The black tapestry hung in heavy folds round the sides of the Cathedral and magnified the impression which its vastness produced. The tapers which surrounded the coffins threw a red and gloomy light over the innumerable multitude which thronged the floor; their receding rays faintly illuminated the farthest recesses, or strained to pierce the gloom in which the summits of the pillars was lost; while the sacred music pealed through the distant aisles, and deepened the effects of the thousand voices which joined in the strains of repentant prayer.'⁴

CHAPTER III

The Tourist Invasion

Madame DE STAEL, with her lover, Rocca, and Albertine, her daughter, left London to return to Paris on May 8th. Most of the friends of her exile were sorry to see her go, feeling that something vital had been taken from their lives. On the evening of her departure Mary Berry wrote, 'I own I much regret her absence. She had a frankness with me, and a power of exciting my mind. Now she is gone, while *I* am regretting *her*, she will never think of *me* till we meet again. I know her well, with all her faults, ridicules, and littlenesses, and yet she is a very superior creature.' Miss Berry did her friend an injustice. Within a fortnight it was Germaine de Staël who was writing to *her*, complaining that she had been forgotten. She had quickly settled down in Paris, exchanging her London entourage of Lords and Dukes for one even more exalted. 'Quel Homme que cet empereur de Russie. Sans lui nous n'aurious rien qui ressemblât à une constitution. Il est à merveille pour moi; il vient chez moi, et il faut que vous soyez assez bonne pour dire cela negligamment aux Russes, afin qu'ils me respectent... Vous n'aurez les souverains, selon mon avis, que vers les premiers jours de juin. L'empereur veut voir la constitution proclammée'.[1] She was referring to the projected visit of the Allied Sovereigns to the court of the Prince Regent, for which London was eagerly waiting.

Another diarist, Lady Charlotte Campbell, took a less charitable view of the departed Frenchwoman. She had also had letters from Paris. 'The Staël is safely lodged there and is to give parties immediately to all the great characters,—the Emperor of Russia, l'Infini, the King of Prussia, l'Impossible, and, in short, the heroes of all ages and principles; with the intention of extracting from them the real quintessence and vital principle of virtue, in a hydrogen state, which she means to have ready in bottles for exportation. N.B.—none are genuine but those sealed with her own arms, viz. gules, two arms akimbo, surmounted by a Saracen's head, sable, crowned with a French pyx; crest, a cock and bull; badge, a cat and bladders. These have all been conferred by Louis XVIII during his last visit to London.'[2]

The Emperor Alexander seemed happy to be invited to interesting houses, such as Madame de Staël's. He had nothing to complain of in his reception by the common people, who rightly gave him most of the credit for Paris having escaped siege and battle, but he was disappointed in his relations with the Royal Family and was beginning to have second thoughts about the wisdom of the Bourbon restoration. The speech Louis had made at Grillon's Hotel, ascribing his return to France solely to the British, had come to his notice. As time went by it rankled more and more. Accordingly he did not scruple to spend time with the Bonapartists and paid visits to Malmaison, where Josephine, Napoleon's former wife, was living in pleasant retirement cultivating her beautiful garden. *The Times* was affronted to learn that he had dined with 'the ci-devant mistress of Barras and her son', 'we are sorry to see that sovereign condescending to such *low* company.'[3] In less than two weeks the same paper had the satisfaction of reporting the sudden death of that lady, 'in consequence of a disorder which at first exhibited symptoms of a catarrhal fever, but suddenly assumed such a

malignant character, that it carried her off in three days.'³
Sir Archibald Alison, who visited Malmaison soon after the
ex-Empress's death, spoke more charitably. Josephine 'passed
the close of her life at . . . a villa charmingly situated on the
banks of the Seine. . . . She lived in obscurity and retirement,
without any of the pomp of court, or any of the splendour
which belonged to her former rank,—occupied entirely in
the employment of gardening, or in alleviating the distress
of those around her. The shrubberies and gardens were laid
out with singular beauty, in the English taste, and contained
a vast variety of rare flowers, which she had for a long period
been collecting. These shrubberies were to her the source of
never-failing enjoyment; she spent many hours in them
every day, working herself, or superintending the occupation
of others; and in these delightful occupations seemed to
return again to all the innocence and happiness of youth.
She was beloved to the greatest degree by all the poor who
inhabited the vicinity of her retreat, both for the gentleness
of her manner, and her unwearied attention to their sufferings and their wants . . . her death occasioned an universal
feeling of regret, rarely to be met with amidst the corruption
and selfishness of the French metropolis.'⁴

Though Paris continued in an abnormal state, a garrison
town full of excitements and dissipations, the countryside of
France was slowly returning to normal;—'the grapes of
Bordeaux no longer rotting on their vines; the looms of
Lyons no longer silent for want of work, the labours of
agriculture no longer carried out only by women and aged
men, the refactory conscripts no longer working in chains
on the high roads, the last hope of the respectable family no
longer dragged from his professional studies to be enrolled
among the guard of honour of a tyrant.'⁵ Meat, vegetables
and dairy produce were being shipped across the Channel
where they occasioned an immediate drop in prices. In

England pork had recently cost eightpence a pound. Pigs
sent from Cherbourg to Portsmouth rapidly reduced the
price to fourpence or fivepence. But the price of bread, the
principal anxiety of the poorer class, showed no sign of
dropping. On May 21st it was announced that a quartern
loaf would soon cost a shilling.

Not all the troops from France were coming home. Some
of the fresher ones were being taken off from ports along the
west coast and shipped to America to pursue the war there.
James Madison, the settlers' president, was rapidly usurping
the role left empty, now that Bonaparte was safe on Elba, of
principal public enemy, and the stock of adjectives thought
up for the Corsican were now being employed for his abuse.
The English were beginning to be worried, too, about the
over-liberal peace terms offered to France, especially the
permitted strength of her army. France was to have 220,000
troops, 68,000 more than in 1792, which many people
thought was madness. And as yet the peace treaty had not
been signed.

No doubts or fears about the future could discourage the
English in their new-awakened passion for travel and sight-
seeing. By Whit Sunday, the day of Josephine's death, there
were reported to be 12,000 English persons in Paris, not to
mention those still on the roads. Mr Ward did not think the
numbers varied much from week to week, for as many went
as arrived.

One pair of travellers on the way were the painters
Benjamin Robert Haydon and David Wilkie, who set out
from Brighton on May 26th, choosing the route to Dieppe
because it was less frequented than the Dover–Calais way.
They paid a guinea and a half each for their passage on a
little sailing ship which started at 9 in the evening with a
load mostly of French officers returning home, 'full of
gaiety, toasts and sentiments',[5] and docked in front of the

Hôtel de Londres at 3 p.m. the next day. They spent a night in Dieppe, their hotel being the cheapest they were to find on their travels. Dieppe was a poor fishing town, the harbour neglected since before the Revolution, the people mostly peasants, but the painters were delighted by the foreignness and by the colourful dresses of the women. The next morning, with a Mr Sewell whom they had picked up on the crossing, they engaged a cabriolet and made their way to Rouen through country which Haydon described as the richest he had ever seen.

Haydon and Wilkie, both in their late twenties, were determined to enjoy themselves; enchanted to be free for a little from irksome family ties. They had set out on an enormous adventure, to a country which had been a legend to them in their childhood. For the first part of their journey they saw everything through rose-coloured spectacles, enjoying the inns and making themselves popular with their un-English enthusiasm for attempting to talk the language. They made none of the criticisms, common to most travel diaries of the time, about discomfort, unaired beds and the need for a coat of paint. 'The inns are the most curious places we have ever seen,' wrote Wilkie to his sister, 'and as we take every opportunity we can of speaking to innkeepers and their servants, our attempts at French have amused ourselves and them so much, that our journey has been a perpetual roar of laughter. In short, we have appeared to be three such merry fellows, even to them, that they have told us they will never forget us. The climate of this country is so delightful that it is impossible not to feel in good spirits; and in addition to this, the wines are so light and exhilarating, that it seems to make it quite a paradise.'[6] David Wilkie's good spirits, enhanced only too frequently by the delightful wines of the country, were to prove an embarrassment to his staider companion on more than one occasion during their holiday.

The entrance to Rouen was impressive and promising, with wide boulevards, planted with beautiful rows of trees, but the older centre of the town was dirty and uncared for and though many of the houses were fine in themselves the streets were so narrow that they could not properly be seen. The two painters decided to venture out to a play on their first evening and were pleasantly astonished to find that they could understand nearly all of it, for it was a version of one they had recently seen in London, 'Love Laughs at Locksmiths'. The people in the streets looked poor and badly dressed, so they were surprised to find themselves part of an audience who wore very fine clothes. 'The acting, considered as a representation of the French character, we could not but consider as extremely natural, and much less extravagant than that generally seen on the English stage.'[6]

Next day was a Sunday, so they went to High Mass at the Cathedral, surreptitiously sketching incidents that caught their eye. The immense building was full, with a variety of costumes, from the ankle-length skirts and tall white head-dresses of the peasant women to the fashionable clothes of the society that had filled the theatre of the previous night. Some of the worshippers were queueing for confession and Wilkie was impressed with their demeanour. He made a drawing of these. 'The awe this produced on us was, however, considerably removed by seeing a number of young men playing at some game, like cricket, immediately before the church. Towards dusk we found the streets crowded with people very gaily dressed, the shops all open, and numbers of raree shows, as jugglers, in the streets to attract attention.' Back at the inn Wilkie showed his sketch to the Landlord's son. '"Ah, ah, la confessional," said the boy, disgusted, "des bêtes, des bêtes,"'[6] showing that the re-awakened appetite for religion in a country where it had been so long prohibited was not universal.

The route to Paris continued through a sunny countryside planted with rye and wheat. They met with a quantity of English sailors who had been captured at the Battle of Trafalgar and were returning home to Portsmouth after being prisoners for nine years. At Ecouis, where they stopped for dinner, they were cordially invited into the house of an old priest. It was here that Haydon saw the first sign of fear and distrust on the part of a royalist Frenchman, for, when he started 'in an English manner' to express his sentiments about the Revolution, the old man stared at him with horror and begged him to speak lower. This priest was one of many Catholics who, when caught by the Revolution, had found it prudent to equip himself with a wife. Haydon described the resulting family and their pleasant home. 'By the fire sat the Grandmother, old, bowed down with age, the Mother an old French lady in a lace cap, smiling as she spoke, with an elegant accomplished satisfaction, delicate, reserved, yet free and open. His wife, a fine youth, and two little children concluded the group... I never saw a family of more kind feeling. They seemed delighted to see an Englishman. They called in all their acquaintance; in slipped one, then another, then he whispered to go to a one, etc. He took me upstairs and showed me a cabinet of stuffed birds.'⁷ Haydon found that all their faces wore an expression of habitual sorrow, and they were seized with an acute pang when he mentioned their dead king.

At Magny, where the travellers stopped for the night, there were peasants dancing in a meadow to the sound of a violin, as if the world had always been at peace. The last day's travel lay through Pontoise and St Denis and over the battlefield of Montmartre, where the Russians had held their final positions before the surrender of the city. Here, though there were no corpses to be seen, the remains of cartridges and wadding were scattered about, as clean and undecayed as on the day of battle because of the dryness of the weather.

The Hôtel Villedot, to which Haydon and Wilkie had been recommended, proved uncomfortable and extravagant in its charges. They decided to take rooms for one night only and go in search of something cheaper. It was not the custom for Paris hotels to supply their guests with meals, so they went out to dine at one of Paris's many *traiteurs*. In a beautiful warm evening they went exploring; to Louis' palace of the Tuileries, with its beautiful garden, to the Place Vendôme, with its empty column sheathed in the melted-down brass of captured cannons, to the Palais Royal, the centre of the city's dissipation and depravity. There were far more people in the streets, they thought, than there would have been in London on a similar evening, the crowds including large numbers of Russian and Austrian soldiers, but everything was quieter than they had expected, 'no one would suppose anything extraordinary had happened.'[8]

They had arrived, though they did not realize it, on a day of historic importance, almost the last in which occupying troops would be seen in the streets. Lord Castlereagh had signed the peace in the early hours of the morning and the Emperor Alexander and King Frederick-William had gone, among a large and cheering crowd, to take their leave of Louis at the Pavillon de Flore in the palace grounds. Before the end of the week the Emperor of Austria would be gone also and all the posts manned by Allied soldiers would have been relieved by the French National Guard. Russian and Prussian troops were beginning their march to the coast, to embark for home from Boulogne.

After some altercation over their passports, which the patron of the Hôtel Villedot had omitted to take to the police until it was nearly too late for them to move, Haydon and Wilkie took their baggage to a comfortable cheap lodging in the Rue St Benoit, off the Faubourg St Germain, with an amiable landlord, M. Lenoble. Wilkie immediately started to practise French on the lady of the house and was able to do it to excellent effect as he found himself so exhausted by the journey and the walking they had done since their arrival that he decided to spend a couple of days resting in his room. 'I sent for *un médecin*, who prescribed for me a bottle of lemonade, mixed with some drug, of course, which, whether effective or not, had at least the advantage of being well-tasted.'[6]

On the day that Haydon and Wilkie arrived in Paris another English traveller, Henry Wansey, set out from Brighton on the packet *Hero*, arriving in Dieppe the next day. He reached Rouen on June 3rd, just in time to hear 200 cannon fired off to mark the signing of the peace. While he waited for fresh horses at the village of Tôtes he met a party of English people returning from a fortnight in Paris. They explained that the shortage of horses was due to the coming visit of the Emperor of Russia and the King of Prussia to London. Most of the post animals had been requisitioned to convey them and their staffs to the coast. Wansey, who came from Manchester, was interested to see the number of cotton factories on the road to Rouen, most of them idle at the moment. One or two had been founded by Englishmen and still bore their names. At Magny he and his companions stopped for breakfast—'fried mackerel, roast veal, large plate of eggs, a pint of crimson wine, and cheese.'[8] There was coffee, also, and the meal came to two francs a head.

Wansey arrived in Paris on Sunday, June 5th. He was more fortunate than Haydon and Wilkie, at once finding a hotel, in the Rue d'Ambois, that was pleasant, clean and reasonable. He went out, with a friend, to dine, finding a *traiteur* among the dozens in the Palais Royal. It was said that there were over 2,500 restaurants and coffee houses in Paris at this time, and a large proportion of these were situated in the old palace of the Orleans family. 'The people,' Wansey wrote, 'now have possession of it as a place of amusement and public resort, and a most delightful spot it is.' Two persons could have an excellent dinner of three or four courses for the equivalent of three and sixpence. 'The Théâtre Français stands in one corner, so you have not far to walk after dinner, and under shelter all the way.'⁸ He was fortunate enough to find Talma playing there on the first evening of his stay, and decided that the excellence of the acting made up for what the theatre lacked in lighting and fresh paint. He wrote home recommending his friends at all costs to make their headquarters near this splendid palace, suggesting that they pass their first night at the Hôtel d'Angleterre in the Rue Montmartre, kept by an English lady, Mrs Brown, to give them time to look for cheap lodgings. Unlike the French hotels, Mrs. Brown's provided a good dinner with a pint of wine for three francs.

The Palais Royal was an immense mass of architecture 'in the form of the Royal Exchange, but five times as large',⁸ enclosing six squares, some of them planted with trees. The ground floors were almost entirely given over to eating houses of various types, all of them dearer than the restaurants in the other parts of the city. Here you could choose among a hundred and fifty dishes, though Englishmen were unable to get roast beef—('the French do not roast, owing to the absence of sea-coal')—or plum puddings, strong beer or porter. They were astonished by the loaves a yard long. The various establishments included the Café de Foi, where politicians went to read the newspapers; the Cabinet Littéraire of M. Rosa, in which British visitors could drink their coffee in 'a spacious reading room exclusively for English papers';⁹ and the astonishing Café des Aveugles, which opened only after 5 p.m., lit by candlelight, and entertained its patrons with a large orchestra composed entirely of blind musicians. Most Englishmen, especially those who had brought wives and daughters, were scandalised by what they saw at the Palais Royal, though a few admitted that there was something to be said for concentrating all the places of ill fame under one roof. Wansey had an innocent eye and no ladies in his company and gave it as his verdict that it was 'the centre of everything that is pleasant and amusing.'[8]

Edward Planta described the place in his new guide book for the use of visitors. The Palais Royal, he wrote, 'affords a scene of mingled splendour and poverty, beauty and deformity, luxury and misery, which defies all description. Under the arcades at one end is a double row of little shops, in which is the most beautiful and fanciful display of jewels, china, prints, books, ribands, clothes, and indeed of every possible luxury. Beneath are subterranean apartments, in one of which a motley assembly is tripping to the music of some wretched performer; in a second an equally ill assorted group are regaling themselves with their favourite liqueurs, from the vin de Burgundie to simple small beer; in a third a number of miserable objects are crowding round the hazard or the billiard table; and if you dare to venture into a fourth, you witness the most disgusting scenes of debauchery and vice. Ascending once more to the arcades, the stranger admires the cleanly and elegant appearance of the restaurateurs, or taverns. . . .

'If the traveller now ascends to the first floor, a different and unexpected scene now breaks on him. He is admitted into the very abode of gaming and ruin. Innumerable rooms open in succession, and all of them crowded, in which every game of hazard or of skill is played. These are authorised by law, they are under the immediate sanction of the government, and contribute largely to its support. Other ranges of apartments ... are appropriated to scientific pursuits. Lectures on every branch of philosophy, and on the Belles Lettres, are delivered almost every hour. Literary societies here hold their meetings; while, perhaps, the neighbouring apartments are occupied by the fashionable impure. The Palais Royal is the favourite and chosen residence of this miserable and degraded class of society.

'If the traveller ascends still higher, he witnesses more deplorable scenes of depravity. Here he finds the lower and more disgusting prostitutes; he is surrounded by shapes of every description, and it is well if he escapes without paying dearly for his curiosity. Such is the Palais Royal. It is a little world. It comprises in it every character, and almost every scene, that can be imagined,—every thing to inform the understanding, and every thing to corrupt the heart. It has not its parallel in any city in Europe, and actual observation alone can convey any adequate idea of its splendour and its seductions.'[10]

Deprived, for a few days, of the companionship of Wilkie, Haydon explored this universe in miniature alone. His reactions were also different from those of the unsophisticated Wansey. The top floors made an indelible impression on him. 'Paris is a filthy hole, and the Palais Royal a pandemonium in the midst of it... After nine never was such a scene witnessed! The whole is illuminated, the walks and gardens which form the Square full of villainy and depravity, stuffed full, that as you enter you feel a heated, whorish, pestilential air flush your cheeks and clutch your frame. The blaze of the lamps, the unrestrained obscenity of the language, the indecency, the bawdy, bloody indecency of the People, bewilder and distract you. Such is the power and effect of this diabolical place that the neighbourhood, like the country around the poison tree of Java, is mad by its vice and infected by its principles.'⁷ A week later he ventured back again and spent an evening observing the gamblers. 'The expressions of disappointment, of agonizing disappointment, of silent, piercing, acute abstraction, of a dreamy, cold, perspiring vexation in some, of a long drawn leer of chuckling pleasure and yet suppressed triumph in others was apparent, was so apparent that no man could mistake what was passing within. Young women were wandering about, losing at one table and gaining at another, and old men and their wives alternately winning, and failing, and then blaming. Never did I see such a scene. Certainly it was a scene of miserable, heated, midnight vice that without the ecstacies of voluptuous abandonment, had all the consequences of that excess. They looked jugged, fagged, worn out creatures, whose whole lives had been passed in one perpetual struggle of opposite passions. Gain was their wish, to this all was sacrificed. Their dress was neglected, they were dirty, and had all the look of dissipated filth. Hardly a word was spoken and [the] only thing that disturbed this hot, secret, silent scene, was the tinkling of the money and the smart crack of the stick as the gamer whacked it into his bank.'⁷

Before the Revolution the Palais Royal had been the residence of the Dukes of Orleans. Louis-Philippe, the present duke, son of Philippe 'Egalité' and grandson of a Bourbon princess, had returned from Palermo, where he had lived since 1809, a fortnight after the Restoration. His pregnant wife was still in Sicily and was to follow him later. Not surprisingly, he did not attempt to settle in the family palace, now so curiously transformed, but went quietly to stay at the Hôtel Grange Batélière. Like his father, he had supported the Revolution for a time, but by the good offices of 'Monsieur' the Comte d'Artois, had now made peace with the King. He called at the Tuileries and was decorated with the Order of St. Louis. The eventual fate of the Palais Royal was yet to be decided.

Peace was proclaimed in Paris on June 1st, the day after Castlereagh had signed it, together with the Emperors, his brother, Sir Charles Stewart, and the Earl of Aberdeen. The heralds' cavalcade went to all the principal squares and gates of the city and read the proclamation to crowds that included a vast number of Britons. The Emperor Alexander and King Frederick-William were on their way to London, their carriages outstripping their two armies as they marched towards Boulogne and Cherbourg to embark for home.

Alison and Frazer-Tytler had been to the Bois de Boulogne two days earlier to watch this enormous force at its last review. 'They were drawn up in a single line, extending at least six miles. The Allied Sovereigns, followed by the Princes of Russia, Prussia, and France, the French Marshals, and all the leading officers of the Allied armies, rode at full speed along the line; and the loud huzzas of the soldiers, which died away among the long avenues of elm trees, as the cloud of dust which enveloped them receded from the view, were inexpressibly sublime.

'The appearance of these troops on parade was such, that but for the traces which long exposure to all changes of weather had left on their countenances, it never could have been supposed that they had been engaged in long marches. They had always marched and fought in their great coats and small blue caps, carrying their uniforms in their knapsacks. On the night before they entered Paris, however, they put them on, and marched into the town in as fine parade order as that in which they had left Petersburg. The Parisians, who had been told that the allied armies were nearly annihilated, and only had a wreck left, expressed their astonishment with their usual levity: "Au moins," they said, "C'est un beau débris."'[4]

The Allied Sovereigns Come to London

ON the night of June 2nd Mr Planta returned to London
bearing the definitive Treaty of Peace and Amity between
his Britannic Majesty and his Most Christian Majesty Louis
XVIII of France. The terms were extraordinarily favourable
to the conquered nation, securing to her the possession of all
the territory she had held in Europe in 1792 and returning
most of her colonies. The rearrangement of her frontiers
gave her some valuable extra territory. She was permitted to
retain two thirds of her ships of war. The signatories of the
treaty bound themselves to meet at Vienna within two
months to arrange the final settlement of Europe. France had
promised Great Britain to suppress the Slave Trade. 'Thus
we have at length formally entered into that state of peace
which has in effect and in substance existed between the two
nations for the last six weeks... We have voluntarily en-
riched a nation against which we were falsely accused with
entertaining a boundless envy and an insatiable hatred.'[1]
The guns from the Tower of London and in the parks roared
out their approbation at one o'clock the next day. The papers
were printing advertisements for new transparencies appropriate to the occasion and to the coming visit of the Allied
Sovereigns.

The Emperor Alexander was not in the best of tempers
when he left Paris. He was unable to attend Josephine's

funeral on June 4th. Since he was already on the road to
Boulogne, but he was reported as having said to her son,
Prince Eugène, 'I do not know but I shall repent of having
reseated the Bourbons on the throne.'[2] He seems to have
made a private resolution to do none of the things, while in
Britain, that the Prince Regent and the Government expected
of him. Louis' speech at Grillon's Hotel was still rankling.

On June 6th he and the King of Prussia landed in Dover
from the British ship *Impregnable*. He behaved politely to
the inhabitants, making them a speech in English and
French. The sovereigns' arrival had been delayed by hazy
weather and they were forced to spend the night in the port.
In London, the Grand Duchess of Oldenburg had spent the
whole day dressed in her best to welcome her brother. The
crowds had been out all day on the roads to the capital, and
it was not surprising that, by 3 p.m. on their second day of
waiting, they 'became quite impatient.' They dispersed
to their houses, however, remarkably docile and good
humoured, after news had been brought that 'their Majesties
had gone up to town two hours before, in a private manner'.[3]

Miss Berry had been feeling unwell that morning and
could not bring herself to venture out till after two, thus
sparing herself some wasted hours. When she did go out it
was to find Charing Cross and Whitehall entirely blocked
and she was told the road was a line of carriages as far as
Dartford. She fought her way to Lady Glenbervie's house.
'In the meanwhile,' as she later discovered, 'the Emperor
was already at the Pulteney Hotel, with his sister, having
entered quietly in Count Lieven's carriage... We saw nothing, nor heard anything except the guns being fired in the
park to announce the arrival of the sovereigns in their apartments.'[4]

Having frustrated the official plans for his reception,

Alexander condescended to make a formal call at Carlton House, where the Prince Regent received him 'in a very private manner.'³ When he was on his way back from this meeting Lady Shelley managed to catch sight of Count Lieven's carriage. She recognized the Emperor from his likeness to his sister. 'He is very gentlemanlike-looking, and complied very gracefully with the wishes of the mob by appearing on the balcony, and bowing repeatedly.'⁵ In spite of glowing reports in the papers, it is unlikely that the Prince was left in the best of tempers after the Imperial visit. Cumberland House had been prepared, at some expense, for Alexander to live in. He declared his intention, however, of moving into the Pulteney Hotel to be with his sister.

The King of Prussia, always under Alexander's influence, had also sneaked into London incognito, but he was content to settle in the place prepared for him—Clarence House in the Mall—with his two sons and his numerous retinue.

At 6 p.m. the frustrated crowd near the Horse Guards was rewarded by the appearance of a person destined to be more popular than any of the crowned heads—Marshal Blücher, driving up in the Prince's open carriage. 'His countenance is most manly and expressive, bearing the effects of the severities he has encountered; the moustachios on his upper lip are exceedingly prominent'. Nothing delights the British public so much as white hair and venerable age, and he was immediately mobbed. No sooner were the gates of Carlton House unlocked than the crowd made a rush at him. 'All restraint upon them was in vain; the two sentinels at the gate with their muskets were laid on the ground, and the porter was overpowered. The multitude proceded up the yard, shouting the praises of Blücher.'³ Colonels Bloomfield and Congreve came out and managed to get the old man safely into the house, but the crowd assembled in Pall Mall now lost all respect for the decorum of the place; they

instantly scaled the walls, and their impetuous zeal on this
occasion was indulged, and the great doors of the hall were
thrown open to them.'³ The Cossack Marshal, Platoff, was
received with similar ecstasy by Londoners, who made continuous efforts to get near and shake him by the hand. Next
morning, when Marshal Blücher went out to see the sights,
the crowd immediately fell upon his carriage, unhitched the
horses and drew him about the streets. When he eventually
descended in an attempt to reach his house, he was again
mobbed and nearly crushed to death. He confessed to Lord
Burgersh that he had never been so frightened in his life.

The illuminations of the month of April had been put on
again with new and splendid additions. At Carlton House
the Regent had invested in some of the new gas lights.
Pulteney's Hotel, which had stolen London's most illustrious
guest from under the royal nose, put up a plain and dignified
sign saying 'Thanks to God'; the Portuguese Ambassador's
house was illuminated 'with its usual costliness';¹ Castlereagh's home in St James's Square had a transparency of a
dove bearing an olive branch; the Covent Garden Opera had
one of Britannia trampling on Napoleon with Elba to be
seen on the horizon. This time it was Akerman's that
attracted the biggest crowds, with a display in gaslights that
outdid all the others.

The Queen had arrived from Windsor to take up residence
at Buckingham House, where she intended to hold a series
of Drawing Rooms. It had been her painful duty to write to
her daughter-in-law, the Princess of Wales, intimating that
her presence at these functions would not be welcome.
Caroline's reply, censored and put into literate English by
her supporter, Samuel Whitbread, had been printed in *The
Times*. The royal quarrel cast a gloom over a situation
already made delicate by the Emperor's tactless behaviour.
On the morning after his arrival Lady Campbell called at

Connaught House and found Caroline 'dressed in a style as if she expected some visitors'.⁶ The Princess confessed she was hoping for a call from one of the visiting sovereigns and had sent her chamberlain to welcome them to London. The King of Prussia had returned the courtesy, but as yet she had had no acknowledgment from Alexander. As gently as she could, Lady Campbell tried to persuade her friend that it was unlikely she would receive any such visits. Caroline cried out unhappily, 'Then the Prince has conquered!' She was in the middle of a letter to the Prime Minister, Lord Liverpool, demanding permission to leave the country. If she could not go abroad, she protested, she would die of despair. She persuaded her friend to put the letter into decent English, and Lady Campbell complied out of pity, though most unwilling to do so for fear she would be accused of having written it.

The London press, like the good-humoured London public, were determined, out of a desire to annoy their own sovereign, to speak nothing but good of the visitors. Incidents such as Alexander's incognito dash to the capital were interpreted as evidence of a charming modesty. 'He has a perfect indifference to show or parade.'¹ Since her arrival in March, the Duchess of Oldenburg had spent every single day in sightseeing and, by this time, knew more about the places of interest in London than almost any of its residents. She was bursting to show it to her brother, and the two of them, rising at an unusually early hour, toured the interesting sights of the city at an astonishing speed. They showed obvious impatience with the programme drawn up for their entertainment and frequently missed appointments or arrived at them scandalously late. Their faults and rudenesses were cheerfully ascribed to a delightful curiosity and an enthusiasm for English life. 'The pursuits of the Emperor Alexander, like those of his sister,.. afford evident proofs of praiseworthy curiosity and good taste... Such is his activity that they who would observe him well, must be at least as early risers as himself.'[1] He walked in Kensington Gardens and Hyde Park; looked over Westminster Hall, the Abbey and the tombs there; visited the British Museum and the Bank of England; explored the city and the docks; went out to Richmond, Hampton Court and to the Ascot races. Before breakfast he would go riding, and a typical morning canter took him across Westminster Bridge to Southwark, and back to his hotel by way of London Bridge, Finsbury Square, the City Road, the New Road and the Edgware Road. The royal brother and sister went everywhere without military escort. On their visit to the docks the people pressed so close to their carriage that the Emperor was forced to lean out and warn them they were putting themselves in danger. His polite anxiety for their safety earned him yells of delight.

The evening entertainments were less to the visitors' taste than the informal sightseeing they crammed into their mornings—formal dinners at Carlton House; at Lord Liverpool's; with the Queen at Frogmore—followed by visits to the theatre where they invariably arrived so late that they missed all but part of the last act. This loss was not so great as might have been supposed, for they could not have heard much of the performance. The arrival of any of the foreigners in a box was a signal for the audience to rise and cheer, drowning what was left of the performance in chatter, queueing with their backs to the stage to get near enough to shake somebody by the hand—Marshals Blücher or Platoff for preference. After a day or two the nerves of the visitors began to suffer. Creevey wrote to his wife, 'Blücher is a very nice old man, and so like your friend Lord Grey that Lady Elizabeth Whitbread cried when she met him at Lady Jersey's. Platoff is so cursedly provoked at the fuss that he won't accept an invitation to go out. To be sure, as Russian is the only language he speaks, I don't much wonder at his

Louis XVIII entering Paris, May 2nd, 1814.

Encampment of the British Army in the Bois de Boulogne.

The Emperor Alexander and his sister visiting Billingsgate market, June 1814.

resolution. They are all sick to death with the way they are being followed about, and, above all, by the long dinners. The King of Prussia is as sulky as a bear, and scarcely returns the civilities of the populace.'[7]

All the same, it was the Prussians, the unsmiling King and the young princes, that Creevey and many members of society preferred. Though Alexander was the darling of the ladies and the crowds in the streets, it was Frederick-William who pleased the gentlemen. It was stated that Bonaparte had expressed the same opinion to some English officers on Elba —'I'll tell you the difference between the Emperor of Russia and the King of Prussia. The Emperor thinks himself a very clever fellow, and he is a damned fool; whereas the King of Prussia thinks meanly of his own talents, and he is a very sensible man.'[7] Frederick-William succeeded in taking the eye of at least one lady. Lady Shelley, watching him go in to the Queen's Drawing-room, pronounced him 'a fine-looking man, apparently not more than thirty years of age. His sons are pleasant-looking boys, and all the suite—as one might have expected—are very soldier-like in appearance.'[5]

Peace had not yet been declared in London, as it had been in Paris, and on the third day after the Sovereigns' arrival a rumour went about that the proclamation would be read that afternoon. It was a beautiful day. Indeed, it had been dry and sunny ever since Louis passed through the capital and it was beginning to look as if peace were inseparable from fine weather. Miss Berry went in an open landau to the gates of St James's Palace and then to Charing Cross. 'In every part the crowd was immense; all met together with the same intention as ourselves, but the peace was not read! It appears to me that the Government ought to have given notice of this, in order that people might not have been disappointed in the hope of hearing so great a blessing announced.'[4] All they managed to see was four or five of the Regent's carriages waiting to convey the King of Prussia to be invested with the Garter at Carlton House.

The Prince Regent's carriages, except when they were occupied by foreigners, excited no pleasure in the streets. He became daily more unpopular and could not stir abroad without provoking trouble. 'Prinny is exactly in the state that one would wish,' said Creevey, spitefully, 'he lives only by the protection of his visitors. If he is caught alone, nothing can equal the execration of the people who recognise him. *She*, the Princess, on the contrary, carries everything before her.'[7] Lady Campbell, however, was not optimistic for poor Caroline. 'I hear that all ranks, except merely those who bask in the sunshine of the Regent's favour, have expressed themselves warmly for the Princess: and that the Prince cannot move out without hisses and groans...but what good will it do her! None, I fear, the most that can happen is having her establishment put on a more liberal footing by the nation,—and then the Princess will go abroad, run into all sorts of foolish scrapes, and be forgotten at best.'[6]

On Thursday, June 9th, an announcement in the press threatened to plunge London's festivities into mourning. It was rumoured from Europe that Wellington, on his way from Paris to Madrid, had been waylaid on the road with his two aides-de-camp, and murdered. The report was mercifully contradicted the next morning.

The next evening, after the sovereigns had spent an afternoon at the Ascot races, a gusty wind got up, strong enough to extinguish some of the illuminations. It was the first break in the perfect weather since peace had become a fact. That night both Lady Campbell and Miss Berry dined with the Princess at Connaught House. Nobody round the table knew, as they ate their dinner, that Caroline and her adviser Whitbread had planned the action that was to provide both press and public with the best gossip of the whole festive

week—her visit to the Covent Garden Opera. Next morning
Lady Campbell was surprised at being sent for again. She
hurried round to Connaught House, where the Princess told
her of the plan and asked her to be in attendance. All had
been carefully plotted, and Whitbread had decided at what
hour her entrance to the theatre would be most effectively
made. He had advised the princess not to allow 'Willikins'
to be of the party—his reference being to young William
Austin, her protégé, and, some whispered, illegitimate son.

The entertainment offered that evening was an Allegorical
Festival, 'The Grand Alliance', followed by the opera
'Richard Coeur de Lion'. In the event it hardly mattered
what spectacle was mounted, as, from the entrance of the
first foreigner, no further attention was paid to the stage.
Special precautions had been taken to reinforce the theatre,
as if against a siege, but these proved insufficient. At 5 p.m.
an immense crowd started to collect and succeeded in batter-
ing down the inner doors and the barrier in front of the pay
box. More than 2,000 people got in without paying for their
seats; the decorations of the theatre were damaged and many
ladies had their dresses torn. The audience became progres-
sively more unruly as they waited for the spectacle to begin
at 8 o'clock, though a wit in the gallery kept them amused
for some time with a demonstration of his skill as a whistler.

The guests had been having one of their tedious long
dinners, this time at Lord Liverpool's, and did not make
their appearance until half past ten. The visiting sovereigns
were in uniform, their hair unpowdered in the modern
fashion, the Prince Regent being the only one of the party
to wear powder. Generals Chernichev and Bülow attended
on their monarchs; Castlereagh and Stewart were in the
royal box. At their entrance the opera stopped and everybody rose to their feet, cheering for several minutes. A special
anthem was sung, followed by God Save the King, repeated

twice. It was during the singing of this that the Princess of
Wales entered another box, 'magnificently habited in black
velvet, with a diadem and plume beaming with diamonds'.[1]
The length of Lord Liverpool's dinner had ruined Whitbread's careful timing. By coming in while the sovereigns'
acclamations were still going on the Princess 'got no *distinct
and separate applause*, though certainly a great deal of what
was going on was directed at her'.[1] Lady Campbell, who was
standing behind Caroline, told the story to her diary. 'When
we arrived at the Opera, we saw the Regent placed between
the Emperor and the King of Prussia, and all the minor
Princes, in a box to the right. "God Save the King" was
performing when the Princess entered, consequently we did
not sit down. I was behind, so of course I could not see the
house very distinctly, but I saw the Regent was at the time
standing and applauding the Grassinis. As soon as the air
was over, the whole pit turned round to the Princess's box
and applauded *her*.—We, who were in attendance on Her
Royal Highness, entreated her to rise and make a curtsey,
but she sat *immovable*, and, at last, turning round, she said
to Lady —, "My dear, Punch's wife is nobody when Punch
is present." We all laughed, but still thought her wrong not
to acknowledge the compliment paid to her; but she was
right, as the sequel will prove.—"We shall be hissed," said
Sir W. Gell.—"No, no", again replied the Princess with
infinite good humour, "I know my business better than to
take the *morsel out of my husband's mouth*; I am not to
seem to know that the applause is meant for me till they call
my name." The Prince seemed to verify her words, for he
got up and bowed to the audience. This was construed into
a bow to the Princess, most unfortunately, I say most unfortunately, because she has been blamed for not returning
it; but I, who was an eye-witness of the circumstances, know
the Princess acted just as she ought to have done. The fact

was, the Prince *took the applause* to himself; and his friends, or rather his *toadies* (for they do not deserve the name of friends), to save him from the imputation of this ridiculous vanity, chose to say that he did the most beautiful and elegant thing in the world, and bowed to his wife!!

'When the Opera was finished the Prince and his supporters were applauded, but not enthusiastically, and, scarcely had His Royal Highness left the box, when the people called for the Princess and gave her a very warm applause. She then went forward and made three curtseys, and hastily withdrew.—I believe she acted perfectly right throughout the evening; but everybody tells the story differently.'[6]

When the Princess's coachman 'attempted to drive home through Charles Street', Lady Campbell related, 'the crowd of carriages was so immense it was impossible to pass down the street, and with difficulty the Princess's carriage backed, and we returned past Carlton House, where the mob surrounded her carriage, and, having found out that it was Her Royal Highness, they applauded and huzzaed her till she, and Lady —, and myself, who were with her, were completely stunned. The mob opened the carriage doors, and some of them insisted upon shaking hands with her, and asked if they should burn Carlton House.—"No, my good people," she said, "be quite quiet—let me pass, and go home to your beds."'[6] She was then allowed to proceed, but the mob followed after her carriage, crying out 'Long live the Princess of Wales! Long live the Innocent!' Lady Campbell observed that Caroline was pleased and touched, but the incident was misconstrued by many people.

Nothing, however, could raise the Princess's spirits for long. Alexander's failure to call on her was a sad disappointment. As Whitbread wrote to Creevey, 'She is sadly low, poor Body, and no wonder. What a fellow Prinny is!'[7]

The Regent, too, was showing only too clearly that he was not enjoying the celebrations. 'All agree,' wrote Creevey to his wife, 'that Prinny will die or go mad. He is worn out with fuss, fatigue and *rage*. He came to Lady Salisbury's on Sunday from his own dinner beastly drunk, whilst her guests were all perfectly sober. It is reckoned to be very disgraceful in Russia for the higher orders to be drunk.'[7]

Lady Shelley took advantage of the Salisbury gathering to observe the royalties at closer quarters, and her reports were less enthusiastic than those of the daily press. 'The Emperor of Russia, and the King of Prussia, appear less well in society, particularly the former, who is shy and very deaf. He has a bad figure, tightened in at the waist, and has a chest like a woman. His epaulettes are large, and placed very forward; and his arms hang in front very awkwardly... He expressed delight at the crush of an English assembly, which he preferred to the stiffness of a Paris circle... The King of Prussia, who has a very short waist, wore the Garter over very loose white pantaloons, and long ill-made boots which looked bad. But his countenance is extremely interesting... The charming Grand Duchess was there, and honoured me by her remembrance... Lady Pembroke (née Woronzow) ...told me that the Grand Duchess's illness arose from her being confined with her youngest child at a palace near Moscow while the city was burning. She has ever since been subject to these dreadful epileptic fits... She was dressed last night in the most magnificent pearls I ever saw—scattered all over her head in large bunches and drops. She wore a necklace of egg-shaped pearls of enormous size. Her shoulders are very like her brother's, whom she closely resembles; but he has not her astonishing quick eye.'[5]

Earlier that Sunday there had been a tremendous gathering in Hyde Park, in which the numbers 'even exceeded the countless multitudes which have filled the streets during the past weeks; to say nothing of the crowds of horsemen and carriages.'[1] Alexander rode out in scarlet uniform with a cascade of feathers falling from his hat. In the morning he had attended Divine Service at the Russian chapel in Welbeck Street, while Frederick-William and his sons had been to a private ceremony at Westminster Abbey. Lady Shelley, at great risk to her neck because of the press of horses, attached herself to the retinue of the allied generals. 'Old Platoff, the Hetmann of the Cossacks, appeared on the scene with two of his attendants, armed with long spears. As he speaks no language but Russ, he is not so much attended as the rest. . . He is a fine-looking man, apparently under 40 years of age, although I am told that he is 64. He rode a white horse, sixteen years old, which he had ridden in all the campaigns. Old Blücher came next, attended by Burgersh and Sir Charles Stewart. He was mounted on the charger which he rode during his campaign, and in all the great battles. His seat is very good and he is the broadest, stoutest old fellow that ever was seen.'[5] Princess Charlotte, her quarrel with the Regent in temporary abeyance, drove in her carriage round the park, looking well and handsome. 'What a strange and galling sight for the Princess of Wales,' Lady Campbell remarked to her diary.

On returning to his hotel to dress for dinner the Emperor took off his hat with the plumes, bowed and shook hands with a number of the enthusiastic ladies who continually lined his path. 'The eagerness to see His Imperial Majesty, which confers so much credit on the taste and feelings of the English, is felt equally by all ranks. Carriages filled with ladies of distinction are ranged along every street through which it is thought he will pass, and even the staircase and passage of the Pulteney Hotel has a temporary erection where ladies admitted by ticket are accommodated in order to witness his arrival and departure to or from his chamber.'

Some ladies came from a considerable distance for this pleasure and Pulteney's did a roaring trade. Far from resenting this invasion of his privacy, Alexander treated the lovesick ladies with the greatest good humour. 'On passing in or out of the hotel, .. he very condescendingly shook hands with some of the females, and would put his hand between the rails of the staircase to shake hands with others.'[1]

CHAPTER V

The Art Treasures of the Louvre

THE day of the Hyde Park review was the feast of Corpus Christi. It was this popular festival, when the people had been used to decorating the streets, that King Louis chose for the return of France to a proper observation of Sunday. For the past twenty years shops had stayed open throughout the week and Sunday had been no different from any other day. Haydon, who had been in Paris for ten days, was able to make a comparison. 'Last Sunday the people were at work, the shops were open, the inhabitants dirty and dissipated. Today the shops were shut, the people happy and clean. No-one can conceive the difference unless they had seen it.'[1] In the course of the day he spoke with 'an old respectable Frenchman' who told him, with shining eyes, 'This is indeed a Sunday, and makes me quiet and composed after the turbulence of twenty years.' As in the days before the Revolution, the Parisians hung out anything colourful they could find—carpets, tapestries, lengths of silk and linen—from the windows of their houses, held in place by pots of flowers and greenery. The cobbles were strewed with branches and scattered with petals and in many streets decorated altars were put up. Some of the English tourists were apprehensive when they heard of Louis' plan, feeling that 'such an alteration was very impolitic in the king, and that it would not be attended to; but the event has shown

that His Majesty has acted wisely. It seemed to be acquiesced
in by every body with pleasure, and very different from the
preceding Sunday. Almost every shop was shut, and the
solemnity of the day has been observed almost as much as in
London.'[2] In the streets everything was 'gaiety and bustle',[1]
with everybody dressed in their smartest clothes.

Louis had set an example, since his arrival, by attending
daily mass in the chapel of the Tuileries. The public was
admitted to the Salle des Maréchaux, a room so named
because it was hung with portraits of Napoleon's eighteen
marshals, to watch him going in and coming out from the
celebration. There was always a crowd to witness this event,
so large on Sundays and holy days that tickets had to be
issued. Preference was always given to the British, by Louis'
express command, and it was only necessary for an Englishman to mention his nationality to have himself conducted to
a place of honour in front of the legitimate ticket holders.
When he caught sight of clothes of a style familiar to him
from his stay across the Channel, Louis would sometimes
stop and invite the wearers to come into the service. On the
day of Corpus Christi Louis went to chapel with his niece
and two of the marshals to shouts of 'Vive le Roi' from a
crowd that included Haydon, Wilkie, Wansey and a number of other Englishmen. He looked smiling and happy, 'a
simple good honest man, with a good healthy colour in his
face',[2] but Wansey thought the Duchesse d'Angoulême
looked dejected.

After watching Louis go to mass, many visitors pursued
their own devotions in the afternoon at the French Protestant
church near the Louvre. The service reminded people of the
Church of Scotland. In the evening an English sermon was
preached by a Mr Smith in a chapel in the Rue St Antoine.
Though the shops were now shut on Sundays the theatres
were permitted to be open and most of the travellers pre-

ferred to finish their day at the play rather than in listening
to the Hell-fire preaching of this 'canting Methodist.'³

On the evening of Corpus Christi the Odeon was staging
Cimarosa's 'The Secret Marriage', the Théâtre Vaudeville a
ballet of 'Cupid and Psyche', while Talma was reviving
Ducis' translation of 'Hamlet' at the Théâtre Français.
Wansey went to 'The Secret Marriage', where he found,
sitting in the audience, that the 'ladies of Paris are very
agreeable and polite to strangers.'³ The painters chose the
Cirque Olympique for their evening entertainment, where
Haydon, unmoved by the amiability of the beauties of
France, was delighted to observe an English woman—
'unaffected, natural, interesting, full and finely formed. O
Heavens, this is the first time I have felt my heart warmed
by the sight of a woman since I entered France. The manners
of the French are fascinating, but I have never seen one yet
without a beard, which destroyed the effect of their sparkling eyes. As to their forms! really, really, skeletons wrapped
up in lace and muslin and fringe. Never did I see the
superiority of my dear, darling countrywomen so decidedly
manifested.'¹

The difference in feminine fashions on the two sides of
the Channel was so great that visitors could be distinguished
from a distance and many a shy English lady was covered
with confusion at the notice she elicited in the street. 'Quelle
tête Anglaise! Quelle figure Anglaise!' yelled the urchins,
dancing along beside them, and their parents were not much
more reticent. Legends about French politeness were quickly
dispelled. 'The English ladies I have seen here,' wrote Wilkie
to his sister, 'look simple and interesting, but the French
ladies tell me that, although they are handsome, their dress
is frightful.'² But Wilkie found the Parisians very ready to
oblige a stranger. As a Scot he was devoid of English stand-
offishness and continued his enthusiastic battle with the

language. 'I used frequently, at first, to ask the way to a place that I knew, to see if I understood their answer. I used, also, to buy some trifle for the sake of getting into conversation; but what I have derived the greatest advantage from is, that of talking to the people of the house we live in. This I found needed only a beginning, for such is the temper of the French people, that they are always willing to listen to you, and to understand what you say. Our hostess is particularly obliging in this respect; she is at all times willing to talk, and so far willing to be understood, that she will repeat what she says over and over again, till I can fully understand her.'[2]

The visitors who knew Scotland were struck by a feature of Paris that reminded them of home. The houses were tall and pretentious in their outside architecture, but 'instead of being in the entire occupation of wealthy and established families, as in a similar situation they would be in the capital of England, they are let out in portions,—the first floors at the rate of six hundred francs a month, (about thirty pounds), the attics at forty francs. Thus, those who can afford to pay three hundred and sixty pounds a year for rent, share their staircases and entrances with the water-carriers, duns, and visitors of those who pay but twenty-five.'[4] These great stone staircases, with their doors communicating to apartments of varying degrees of grandeur and squalor were exactly such as were found in Edinburgh. John Mayne, an Irish lawyer, shared with his parson brother and his wife a 'sitting and dining room and two bedchambers, for which we are to pay five louis a week'[4] in one of these great houses. 'The rooms are low and dark, but neatly furnished; in London they would be considered magnificent. The drawing-room is hung with good prints. Ornamental clock on the chimney-piece, two large looking-glasses in each room, panels of looking-glass in the bedroom doors, plate glass windows, marble tables, beautiful breakfast china—all this sounds well; but the doors are badly furnished, and painted in the commonest manner, a rough iron bolt supplies the place of a lock and is raised by a large key that always stands in the key-hole, the chairs are indifferent, and the floors of tile or brick. The entrance is across a spacious court, and the staircase, being common to the whole house which contains many families, is covered with filth of every kind.'⁴ It was the custom for visitors accommodated in lodgings of this kind to engage a valet-de-place, who did certain chores disdained by the landlady, making the beds and tidying the bedchambers 'even of the ladies', and running errands in the city. The Maynes engaged one 'without a syllable of English' and paid him at the rate of five francs a day. These fashionable lackeys were not invariably to be relied on.

The rate of exchange was improving every day. Shortly after his return to London with the peace treaty, Edward Planta, of Sir Charles Stewart's staff, published his 'New Picture of Paris.' He advised his countrymen how to make the necessary financial arrangements. They should deposit a sum of money at a London banker which was in the habit of transacting business with Paris. Messrs Coutts and Co. and Messrs Hammersley & Co. of Pall Mall were recommended. Most London banks issued letters of credit on Peregaux & Co. This house, in the Rue Mont Blanc, became the first objective of countless foreigners after they had obtained lodgings and taken their passports to be registered with the Bureau de Police. The office of Mr Philips in that bank had become a sort of club for English travellers, where advice could be had, rendezvous made, and a list was kept open for inspection of all Britons present in the city. It was in connection with his visit to this house that one of *The Times* correspondents, newly arrived, had an experience that must have unnerved him more than he was ready to admit.

'I had hired a *valet-de-place*, and, as I thought my first

step should be on Peregaux' head, I desired him to take me
there, saying I had a letter of credit. He accordingly took me
to a magnificent house, where I was informed the master
could not be seen before two o'clock. I thought this rather
strange for a banker, however, at that hour I went, and after
passing through twenty different doors, with a great deal of
whispering among the different attendants, I was ushered
into a small room, in which was sitting a Gentleman with a
sallow complexion and eyes like diamonds. I delivered my
letter to him, which he read, and looking very earnestly,
said, "Well, sir, what do you want me to do in this business?" I thought this rather impertinent from a man who
had my money; but it turned out that the stupid *valet-de-
place* had not taken me to Peregaux, but to Talleyrand-
Périgord, Duke of Benevente! This was an awkward mode
of introduction to this celebrated man, whose great talents
are discoverable in every line of his countenance.'[5]

At the time of Planta's writing the rate of exchange made
one English guinea equal to one louis or twenty-four francs.
The louis had previously been the napoleon, which had consisted of twenty francs only. This change in the currency
gave a splendid opportunity to rapacious landlords and shop-
keepers to trap the unwary. They would bargain first in
napoleons, and later insist in being paid in louis, and many
visitors found to their cost the wisdom of agreeing all prices
in francs rather than in the ambiguous larger coin. In spite
of protracted arguments, John Mayne and his brother found
themselves twenty francs poorer than they thought they had
bargained for at the end of a week in their magnificent
rooms.

Englishmen fell rapidly into the French habit of eating a
light luncheon à la fourchette at about 11 a.m. and dining at
5.30 or 6 p.m. at one of the many *traiteurs* before going to
their evening's entertainment. They were astonished by the

speed at which any of the 250 different dishes advertised in the bills of fare could be produced. Mayne concluded that the price of an average meal was higher in Paris, but that if you wanted a really luxurious dinner you could have it at half what it would have cost in London. Good wines were to be had at a reasonable price; coffee without milk came after the meal, with small glasses of eau de vie. This was the end of drinking for the day and nothing surprised the Englishman so much as the sobriety of the French. Many diarists remarked with astonishment on not having seen a single drunken person in the streets during the whole of their holiday in France—a state of affairs that contrasted sharply with conditions in the towns and villages of England.

Indeed the civilised behaviour of the lower orders in a country most Britons had been taught to think of as barbarous caused much wonder, and nothing more than the high level of literacy. Morris Birkbeck, who travelled to observe the state of agriculture, was astonished to find a peasant woman reading a translation of Young's 'Night Thoughts' as she sat behind the counter of her little tavern, 'This was more than we should have expected in a village alehouse in England.'[6] Another traveller noticed a girl by a market stall studying Voltaire between serving customers. Birkbeck also remarked on the fact that you never saw a Frenchwoman idle; even as she served her shop or tended her animals at market she would have her hands occupied at spinning or knitting or picking hemp. He made a small list of the matters in which the French excelled the English.

'Their drinking no healths, and their temperance in general.

'Their great propriety of manners, and general politeness; including all ranks, but most remarkable in the lowest.

'Their good treatment and excellent condition of their unmutilated horses, of every sort.

'The activity and consequent good health of the women.

'The superior condition of the labouring class; and, as set off against some political grievances, exemption from tithes, poor-rates; and, in comparison, from taxes.'

He made a somewhat longer list of the things that pleased him less.

'The habit of spitting up and down their houses and churches, not confined to the gentlemen.

'The abominable custom of cheapening every article in dealing. . .

'The cabinets d'aisance; and, in some places, the utter want of them.

'The streets, without flag causeways.

'The frequent discharge from the windows.

'The sabots, or wooden shoes.

'The ceremony at meeting or parting—a little overdone.

'The perfect abruptness with which domestics, male, or female, enter your chamber on all occasions.

'Their long meals, and countless dishes. . . .

'The immense standing army, and the increasing number of priests.'[6]

Birkbeck was delighted to see a French gentleman, who presumably had failed to find one of those elusive cabinets d'aisance, arrested for relieving himself in the street. The gendarme, by way of punishment, relieved the offender of his hat.

David Wilkie had come to Paris principally in the hope of selling some of his prints in the art shops that abounded there. He took them round to the gallery of M. Colnaghi, junior, who endeavoured, without much success, to assist him in the matter. After the privations of a long war, the Parisians had not much money or interest to spare for pictures like 'The Village Politicians' or other sketches of life in Britain. Wilkie's secondary objective, and Haydon's principal one, was to see the art treasures looted by Napoleon from the European cities he had conquered, most of which were still being exhibited in the Musée Central des Arts, formerly the Palais du Louvre.

The great building had been scrubbed and scraped as part of Napoleon's plan to beautify Paris—'when he approved of a building,' wrote Mayne, 'he immediately ordered it to be scraped from top to bottom, and a profusion of bees, eagles and capital Ns to be inserted between the parts of the old work. By the time these orders were carried into execution, the building looked quite new and, the work corresponding with that on the buildings erected by him, strangers were effectually deceived; and even the good people of Paris themselves, daily viewing the progress of the workmen, were at last thoroughly convinced that they were indebted for the work to their Great Emperor.'[4] The reconditioned Louvre still shone splendidly white, startling visitors used to the dinginess of London's stone. Seacoal hardly being used in France, the purity of the air in French towns was greatly envied. The exhibition was only open to the public on two days of the week, when an immense multitude would crowd through the gates. Visitors quickly discovered that here, as at the Tuileries, it was only necessary to reveal their nationality to the door-keeper for all restrictions to be brushed aside. It was far pleasanter to go over the enormous galleries when they were practically empty and it was not difficult to obtain permission to make sketches of the magnificent statues on the ground floor (the fig-leaves, insisted on by the Vatican, removed by order of Napoleon) or copies of the rare paintings exhibited in the rooms above. A first view of the main gallery was inclined to be bewildering. Haydon was disappointed—'It is too long—it has too much the look as if one was looking in at the wrong end of a spy glass,'[1] but before long he had acclimatised himself to the grandeur of the room and was able to examine and wonder at the individual works of art. The room measured 1,300 feet and housed 950 paintings—the Italian school, including works by Michaelangelo, Correggio, Guido, Guercino, Julio Romano, da Vinci, Raphael, Salvator Rosa, Veronese and Titian; the Flemish and German schools, with pictures by Gerard Doü, Dürer, Vandyck, Van Eyck, Holbein, Jordaëns, van der Meulen, Ostrade, Rembrandt, Rubens, Teniers, Vandervelde, and Wouvermans; and the French collection, comprising works by Le Brun, the two Poussins, Sueur, the Vanloos, Verney and Vouêt. Raphael's 'Transfiguration' was on its way back to the Vatican, but there was no noticeable hurry to return the other spoils of war, some people, even among France's ex-enemies, arguing that there was something to be said for having all Europe's art under one roof. Haydon and Wilkie were especially impressed with Correggio's 'Marriage of St Catherine' and Veronese's 'Marriage at Cana'. In the opinion of some critics, the gallery was 'by no means well adapted for the purpose to which it is devoted. The cross-lights render it almost impossible to see the pictures, and with regard to many of them it is quite impossible to catch their beauties... To please the vanity of the multitudes of Paris, who flock to view their pillage, a long avenue, with pictures forming its sides, like so many regularly planted trees, may be best adapted; but the persons of taste and feeling would be most touched and gratified, by a distribution into different rooms, where a sort of precedency might be observed, by means of which, natural distinctions might assist the judgment, and prevent that bewildering of the senses which is produced by a vast promiscuous assemblage.'[7]

The sightseers were more uniformly impressed with the contents of the sculpture galleries, if only with wonder at the vast tonnage of stone and marble the ci-devant Emperor had caused to be brought from all over the continent for his glorification. In the Gallery of Antiques, among eight great pillars from the nave of the church at Aix-la-Chapelle, were statues of Demosthenes, Trajan, Menander and Posidippus, all looted from Rome. The Salle des Saisons, named from the painted ceiling of Romanelli, held the fauns, satyrs, bacchantes and rural deities; the Venus rising from her bath discovered near Salone; Flora, with flowers in her hand; Cupid and Psyche, the property of Cardinal Albani, and the famous statue of the boy taking a thorn out of his foot. The Salle des Romans had busts of Brutus, Scipio Africanus and Augustus, and statues of the Roman Matron and the Dying Gladiator, under a painted ceiling of scenes from Roman history. The most famous and admired of all the sculptures were in two smaller rooms—the Laocoon with his two sons, wrestling with the serpent; the Apollo Belvedere, and Napoleon's most recent acquisition, the Venus de Medici.

Perhaps the most notable of all the conqueror's spoils, the bronze horses from St Mark's in Venice, were not housed in the Louvre but could be seen from the windows of its upper galleries, standing on top of the unfinished Triumphal Arch in the Place du Carousel. He had started building this at the time of his marriage to the Austrian princess. Walking home from the theatre one night, Haydon caught sight of this last monument of the conqueror 'towering darkly against the twilight sky,' and could not help thinking 'how little good all his industry had done to the world or himself. All his monuments will serve now but to remind one of his folly, and his vice, his cruelty and tyranny.'[1]

Wilkie's efforts to make copies at the Louvre were singularly unsuccessful. He tried to make a study from Raphael's 'Madonna and Child', but, though he was working on a day when the gallery was closed to the public, so large a number of the 12,000 English reputed to be in Paris were also there

that he gave up. He could not draw with people looking
over his shoulder. On his next visit he tried the sculpture
gallery, but the absence of anything to sit on made him
quickly abandon the attempt to sketch the kneeling Venus.
While he was looking over the statues he was accosted by a
young French artist who, after making searching enquiries
into the state of art in England, invited him to visit the life
class at the Paris Academy. Accordingly he went with
Haydon to the Palais des Beaux Arts, 'and with some difficulty found out the Academie Vivante. This was in a small
disagreeable looking apartment, to which we entered
through a still more disagreeable hall or ante chamber,
where an old woman was stationed to take charge of hats,
great coats, portfolios, etc. The Academy room, which was
not very large, was filled with students of all ages, and
seemingly in all conditions of life. The figure they were
studying from was an old man, and of a much worse character in point of form than any I ever saw in our Academy in
London. They never have any females in their Life Academy;
& if they had, the Academy would require to be conducted
in a very different way, for it would seem to be open to
every body.'² Wilkie's companion was even more disgusted
than he was, and dismissed the Academy with one line of his
diary—'Never did I witness such a dirty set of rooms, filthy,
& the people worse.'¹

The Luxemburg Palace housed an exhibition of paintings
by Rubens, but the four huge pictures of Napoleon's victories
by David had been covered with roughly tacked sheets of
greenish canvas, to the annoyance of visitors who came in
search of art. David's own painting-shop was in the Sor-
bonne, 'which was neither more nor less than an old
church'.¹ Here the vast canvases of 'Napoleon declared
Emperor' and 'Napoleon crowning Josephine' could be
seen, both of interest to the curious for the number of con-

temporary portraits they contained. Wilkie and Haydon went on to look at the works of Gérard, one-time pupil of David, who had leapt to fame with his portrait of Letitia Bonaparte—Madame Mère—and had painted all the leading figures of the Empire. He was now busy putting the Allied sovereigns and generals on canvas and at this exhibition the ex-Emperor and Marie-Louise hung side by side with a new portrait of the Emperor of Russia and Gérard's latest painting, Louis XVIII sitting in Napoleon's study. His excellent likenesses disgusted Haydon, whose mood was daily becoming sourer, 'there is no feeling in his characters or colour,— wretched, smooth, green and blue mud and filth, flimsy and varnishy things. I felt sick, heartily sick, and disgusted.' His description of Gérard's portrait of Napoleon showed him, for all his protests, to have been considerably affected by the painter's power. 'Great God, what a [picture] Heavens, a horrid yellow for a complexion, the tip of the nose tinged with red, his eyes watery; dull, fixed, stern, tiger-like, lurid fierceness; his lids reddish and his mouth cool, collected and resolute.'[1]

One of the King's first duties on his Restoration had been to sit to Baron Gérard, who had painted him sideways to the canvas at a useful-looking desk in a book-lined room of the Tuileries. In spite of the medals and the large epaulettes of his uniform coat, Louis looked very much an English country gentleman of the early nineteenth century, in striking contrast to the Roman splendours, the laurel wreaths and dramatic attitudes of the portraits of the fallen regime. It was hard to believe that the two last rulers of France inhabited the same century.

Once due honour had been done to the dead King, Louis was making regular weekly visits to the theatres, dragging the unwilling but dutiful Duchess d'Angoulême, who had no taste for frivolous entertainments, with him. The

Coronation had been planned for August 25th, the fête of St Louis. Madame de Staël wrote to Miss Berry of the boredom that had descended on the city since the royalties had forsaken it for London. 'Nous sommes ici dans un calme plat. Quant à la société, elle est encore nulle, il s'en rassemble quelque débris chez moi, mais il n'y a point d'ensemble.'[8] A good many of the tourists had left to see the fun in their own country, but she hoped the coronation would bring another flood of them across the Channel. On Elba, the ci-devant Emperor was reported to have gone mad, his physicians despairing of a cure. The English papers, read by the remaining visitors some days late at Peregaux or at M. Rosa's Cabinet Littéraire, spoke mystifyingly of discontents and insubordinations in the French capital, but Henry Wansey, writing to a clergyman in England on the eve of his departure, said that he 'could not hear of any such'.[2] He watched the Fête Dieu processions on June 19th, which seemed to equal those of Corpus Christi in fervour, and felt certain there could be no counter-revolution in favour of Bonaparte—'his date is out.'[3] He did not think the King was making enemies; the government was well supported by strong men like Talleyrand, Fouché and the Abbé Montesquiou. As for the French people, he thought them children still, frivolous at heart, and at the moment revelling happily in the unaccustomed delights of peace.

CHAPTER VI

The Departure of the Allied Sovereigns

WHILE the English papers were making questionable reports of unrest in Paris, the French ones had even odder tales to tell of Britain. *The Times* translated:—'The prisoners lately arrived from England give very curious details with respect to the anxiety of the inhabitants to impress on their illustrious visitors the highest idea of the opulence and prosperity of their country. It is well known that in general the houses of the poorest peasants in England have an air of comfort and neatness too rare in other countries; but exertions were made to improve even on their usual aspect. On the whole road from Dover to London, there was not a ruinous house but was repainted and whitewashed. Doors and windows were newly painted, and the greater part of the ruins completely refurbished. The inhabitants in easy circumstances clubbed together to assist the poor. All sorts of vegetables, flowers and even fruit trees were transplanted to the gardens adjoining the highroad to augment the aspect of fertility and good cultivation.'[1]

The weather in London had been overcast and thundery since the evening of June 10th when the royal visitors had been to the Ascot races, but the sun shone out again on the 13th at the very moment when they boarded a barge to be rowed down the river to Woolwich, evoking a cheer from the crowd. The barge rivalled Cleopatra's—'gorgeously gilded"[1]—with an awning of purple silk embroidered in gold. Lady Shelley stood on a balcony in Whitehall and saw the Emperor of Russia, with his sister and the King of Prussia, go aboard, attended by the Regent and Lord Castlereagh. The water was covered with small craft, barges, gigs from the men-of-war anchored in the river, and scores of little boats loaded to danger-point with spectators. Two large bands accompanied the flotilla on barges, playing alternately.

At Woolwich, a cold collation was served in a magnificent marquee, and then Colonel Congreve, the artillery expert, gave the signal for his demonstration. 'At about 200 yards N.E. of the mound where the royal visitors were stationed, a quantity of compositions placed on three pieces of timber, exploded, producing columns of flame awfully grand. The discharge produced a volcanic appearance, attended by a tremendous roaring; but the burning property of the material was most remarkable. After the discharge, the timber remained in flames, and actually consumed to a cinder. The next display was of the rockets used in besieging... They were fired from the opposite bank of the Thames horizontally over the low grounds, to the distance of 800 or 1000 yards. It is impossible,' went on the reporter of *The Gentleman's Magazine*, 'to describe the effect produced by these discharges. Wonder was expressed by the beholders. The shells thrown by the rockets flew to the distance required, and exploded with horrible sounds. There can be little doubt that a single volley would disunite a body of cavalry. Against that description of force they are peculiarly operative, as they not only kill but spread terror among the horses.'[2]

The Emperor was interested in the rockets, and his sister, always curious about the wonders of science, enjoyed the bangs more than the strains of music that accompanied them wherever they went. But the royal visitors were heartily sick of organized entertainments and their public manners were showing signs of strain. The day after the Woolwich display they went to Oxford, where the Duchess offended everybody by having Dr Crotch stopped the moment he struck up an organ voluntary in their honour. She and her brother were lodged at Merton College, where they 'disdained to occupy the fine beds prepared for them, but passed the greater part of the night à causer: they then threw themselves on the floor until daybreak!'³ Alexander was not impressed with Oxford. He did not care for Gothic architecture. Blenheim was much more to his taste, being his idea of what a nobleman's house ought to be. His verdict on the English and their houses was—'Que les Anglais étaient une nation de princes, qui vivaient dans des cabanes.'³ Though bored with official duties, Alexander did not lack energy for the things that amused him. He returned to London the next night, driving with his sister through the dark in an open carriage, though a thunder-storm was raging overhead. They did not reach their hotel till 3 a.m., but he did not retire to bed. He changed his sodden clothes and rushed out to dance at Lady Jersey's ball until 6. He was up again by 10 and out to St Paul's to see 600 charity children from the parishes of London assemble for a service. Later he took his sister to a cold luncheon at the Mint, where they spent some hours learning the mysteries of coinage.

That evening Lord Castlereagh gave a dinner in his house in St James's Square, after which the guests were to honour Edmund Kean with a visit to Drury Lane to see his 'Othello'. The sovereigns sat down with the Dukes of York, Clarence, Kent, Sussex and Cambridge; Prince Metternich, the Austrian representative, and Prince Hardenburg; the Duc d'Orleans, who had just arrived on an embassy from Paris; the Princes of Prussia, Würtemburg, Weimar and Saxe-Coburg. The Prince of Orange was also present, having

been told, that very afternoon, that his suit to Princess
Charlotte had been finally rejected. As usual, the dinner was
excessively long, with the result that the royal guests did not
appear until the Shakespeare play was finished. At half past
ten, just as the 'tedious afterpiece' 'The Woodman's Hut'
was beginning, they entered their box to shouts of applause
from the audience. The press commended their patience in
sitting out the show, 'in which there was nothing but Miss
Kelly's acting which could rescue our stage from utter con-
tempt',[1] and remarked that it was fortunate that frequent
demonstrations from the public distracted them from what
was happening on the stage.

It had been the firm decision of Prinny's wife to make a
second public appearance at this performance, but her ally
and adviser, Samuel Whitbread, had now developed cold
feet. The repercussions of her Covent Garden visit had
alarmed him. The question of her income was about to come
before Parliament and he did not want to prejudice her chances. Caroline complained to Lady Campbell—'It is not the
loss of the amusement which I regret, but being treated like
a child, and made the puppet of a party.'[4] Covent Garden
had refused to reserve a box for her on future occasions and
she felt insulted at being offered the window of a private
house to watch the procession to the Guildhall dinner when
she felt she ought to have been a part of it. The public's
attitude was some comfort. When she went out in her carriage 'a decently dressed and respectable looking country-
man' came close to the window and said, 'God bless you!
We will make the Prince love you before we have done with
him!' The Princess Charlotte was followed by a mob, crying,
God bless you, but never forsake your mother.'[4]

The Allied Sovereigns' visit was drawing to a close. Peace
was at last to be proclaimed in London on Monday, June
20th, nearly three weeks after its proclamation in Paris. On

Sunday, after a service in the Russian chapel, Alexander went to a meeting of the Society of Friends in St Martin's Lane. The Quakers had made a public statement disassociating themselves from the public rejoicings and deploring those illuminations which showed Britannia triumphing over her enemies. Joy at the end of hostilities was legitimate, but never triumph. To celebrate victory implied a tolerance of war. Besides, the wastefulness of the display could only provoke public dissipation, intemperance and riot. They were unhappy, too, about the provisions of the treaty, which they considered had not done enough towards the suppression of slavery. The Tzar was a man easily swayed by anyone who could preach at him with real religious fervour and he kept open house at the Pulteney Hotel for the Quakers, as well as for deputations from any other religious bodies that cared to call on him. The magnanimous Alexander, who had refused to humiliate his enemies, appeared to British evangelical sects as a more promising leader than any their own royal family could produce.

The Queen came up from Windsor to say goodbye to the foreign guests, and Fanny d'Arblay, her one-time lady-in-waiting, found herself called a second time out of the seclusion of family mourning to attend a Drawing-room at Buckingham House. She wrote to her husband in Paris, 'Hier j'ai quitté ma retraite, très volontiers, pour indulge myself with the sight of the Emperor of Russia. How was I charmed with his pleasing, gentle, and so perfectly unassuming air, manner and demeanour! I was extremely gratified, also, by seeing the King of Prussia, who interests us all here, by a look that still indicates his tender regret for the partner of his hopes, toils and sufferings, but not of his victories and enjoyments. It was at the Queen's Palace that I saw them, by especial and most gracious permission... The Princess Charlotte looked quite beautiful. She is wonderfully improved. It was impossible not to be struck by her personal attractions, her youth, and splendour... I was admirably placed for the view, where every one passed close to me, yet without my being *en evidence*.'⁵

The gentle Fanny was more charitable to the Emperor than some ladies of the court, but then she had only seen him once. After a fortnight of regal entertainments, Lady Shelley was thoroughly disillusioned. 'If I have been led away by the popular cry in favour of the Emperor of Russia, let me now retract my opinion. Each succeeding day dispersed the halo of glory with which fancy had exalted the magnanimous Alexander. Reality, and a nearer approach proves him to be a foolish, good natured, dancing Dandy. Although he has more good qualities than bad, he is but a weak, vain coxcomb. Personally, he is as brave as a lion, but entirely under petticoat government. His sister, the Grand Duchess, has complete power over him; and, shocking as the notion is to English morals, is generally regarded as his evil genius.

'Although the Grand Duchess is very fascinating, she remained in England rather too long for my enthusiasm about her to endure. The other day, in spite of the well-known repugnance of the gallant cits. of London, she insisted on accompanying the Emperor to dinner at the Merchant Taylor's Hall; and, afterwards to the Guildhall. At the dinner she was the only female present. At the Guildhall the cits. were prepared for her being of the party. Although her antipathy to music is well known, the cits. would not omit the National Anthem...

'Long before the departure of the Sovereigns public curiosity had been completely satisfied, and their stay became, at last, a positive nuisance. When the date for their return home was fixed, the joy felt by the higher ranks of society was universal.'³

Be this as it may, there seemed to be no lack of public

interest in the final celebration, the military review in Hyde Park on the day of the peace proclamation. Though Lady Bury was up early she could not get near enough to distinguish any of the individuals who rode by to inspect the troops. 'Every tree in the park was heavily laden with persons of various descriptions, and the balconies, windows, and roofs of the houses fronting the Park were crowded with a great assemblage of beauty and fashion.'³ The loudest shouts were undoubtedly the ones that greeted Platoff and his Cossacks, and old Blücher, the public's special hero. The review was so prolonged that the heralds, who had assembled at 11 a.m. to read their proclamation, were not able to start their tour of the city until after 4. Peace was declared at St James's Palace, Charing X, Whitehall, Temple Bar and Chancery Lane. Though the heralds' procession was not so splendid as the one that had been seen in the Park, 'the pleasing association of ideas which it could not fail to produce in the minds of the spectators amply compensated for this deficiency.'¹

Early on Wednesday, June 22nd, Alexander sent for M. and Mme. Escudier, proprietors of the Pulteney Hotel, to thank them for the attention they had showed to him and to his sister. The Reverend Mr Smirnoff, of the Russian chapel, presented Madame with a handsome brooch as a memento of the visit. The usual crowd had assembled in the street and as Alexander stepped outside to his carriage a lady handed him a beautiful rose. He thanked her graciously and placed it in his sister's bosom. They drove off to the accompaniment of cheering. Baron Nicolai waited till his master was safely out of London before he went round to Connaught House. Poor Caroline had never quite given up hope that she might receive a royal visit, but all she got was a letter, coldly polite, at the hands of the Baron. The Emperor regretted that he had not called, but, 'under the existing circumstances, delicacy only allowed him to express his high consideration.'[4]

It was a beautiful June day when the foreign kings and generals who, for the past two weeks had been the continual object of London's curiosity, drove down through Surrey and Hampshire for their final engagement, the naval review at Portsmouth. All the way from the Thames to the coast people had put up booths and tents; branches of oak, elm and laurel festooned the front of houses, and people came from miles around on foot or in carriages or piled into farm carts. As on the day of the visitors' arrival the roads were lined with 'humble rustics crying out for Alexander and Blücher'[1]; as on the day of their arrival, these multitudes were doomed to wait in vain and then make their way home disappointed. Nobody could discover by what route Alexander and Frederick-William slipped into Portsmouth unobserved, but they arrived after dark and too late for the fine banquet laid on for them at Government House. The people of the port, many of whom had spent the day sitting all over their rooftops, had to be content with the sight of their own least popular royalty, the Prince Regent, who was brought in by a procession of 42 ropemakers in white vests, nankeen breeches and neat round hats, with broad gentian ribbons over their shoulders and white wands in their hands. Since he presented the only diversion of the day, Prinny received a cheer of unaccustomed geniality. The press, on this occasion, was noticeably less ready to attribute the non-appearance of the sovereigns to charming modesty.

The review was magnificent and restored the good humour of the citizens of Portsmouth. The Emperor always showed up best when allowed to mix with ordinary people. He took his sister to the lower deck of the *Impregnable* to watch the crew being issued with their midday ration of spirits. 'He made enquiries concerning it, and asked what quantity of water was added to the rum. Being told that the proportion of water was 6 to 1, a tar observed that it would be no worse for being stronger. Alexander requested the usual allowance and drank it off readily, smiling, and adding his approbation of the liquor, "which", said His Majesty, in very intelligible English, "you call grog, and I think it very good." He had a smaller quantity poured out for the Duchess, who drank it with very much good humour. The men were ordered an extra allowance.'[2] The Regent declared the spectacle of the ships, passing in review on a sea only slightly flecked with white wavelets, to be the grandest he ever saw; the Grand Duchess bore the firing of cannon with 'much fortitude'; the 'amiable and meditative Frederick was wrapped up in the sublimity of a spectacle so new to him; .. the young German princes were quite enraptured; the veteran leaders of horses contemplated, with the firmness becoming to their martial character, an exhibition of a sort to which they had hitherto been perfect strangers.'[2]

When the royalties came ashore in the evening it was to find that Portsmouth had gone mad with joy. They were met with delighted yells of 'Wellington!' Arrived from Paris the day before, the new-made Duke had driven down from London to pay his respects to the Regent, in an open carriage drawn by six greys. These had been unhitched by the young men of the city, who pulled him in triumph to the door of Government House. He was called to the balcony again and again.

Wellington's return to England was the signal for another round of celebrations, though many people felt with Lady Shelley that they had had enough and were longing to settle down to normal life. While the Emperor of Russia was landing back on European soil, Wellington was making his first appearance in the House of Lords, where, in a modest maiden speech, he attributed his military successes to the excellent support he had received. The House then went on to ordinary business, its first debate being on the failure of the treaty to deal effectively with the Slave Trade.

Next morning the papers were full of reports of a great Fair to be held in London in July to honour the victorious general. Many were disgusted. 'We are as proud as the most admiring of his countrymen of the Duke of Wellington's glories, but pronounce it a very odd taste, to think of celebrating military feats in a great fair.' *The Times* begged the organizers to think again. 'They are doing a great injury to the morals of the people, to the comfort of private families, and the regular concerns of trade. Sober minded people are already turning up their noses at such trumpery stuff.'[1]

The Duke, in the meanwhile, was unable to move in London without being mobbed by enraptured crowds. His appearance with Blücher, who had stayed after his sovereign's departure, threatened to bring traffic to a standstill. They came out together from a levee at St James's Palace, 'when they got to Pall Mall the crowd that followed them had increased so much that they could scarcely move; upon this one of the multitude, a strong resolute fellow, exerted himself, and made a lane for them to pass; the huzzas were incessant.'[1] They went together to the opera, where they succeeded in stopping the show. On July 7th Wellington drove to St Paul's in a carriage with the Regent and sat on his right hand for a service of thanksgiving. The next day the Prince gave a banquet for him. Miss Berry was at Lord Castlereagh's that evening, and as she was leaving she ran into some of Prinny's guests coming back merry with drink. 'At the foot of the staircase we met Blücher, who came with Lord Stewart from a dinner at Carlton House, and Blücher, being the worse for it, had great difficulty in getting upstairs. He wished to be introduced to me; he shook hands,

Caricature of an English Officer by Carle Vernet.

"Voila, les Anglais!" English fashions seen by the women of Paris, *c.* 1814.

having been taught here that this was the height of politeness and fashion.'⁶

In the course of the same week Wellington's cousins, the
Wellesley-Poles, gave a banquet for him at their house at
Wanstead, where, for the first time, he came under Lady
Shelley's adoring gaze. It was the beginning of an acquaintance which was to cause Lady Granville to remark, a year
later, that 'Sir John and Lady Shelley ran after the great
Duke in a very disgusting manner, but, as they were together,
sans peur et sans reproche.'⁷ It was one of the pleasantest
evenings, with Prinny, now that his rival sovereigns were
safe across the Channel, restored to good behaviour. After
the royal toasts had been drunk he rose to his feet, between
his own garlanded bust and that of the Duke, and proposed
Wellington's health 'in a very neat speech.' Lady Shelley
gazed across the table at her hero as he got to his feet to
reply—'he had a broad smile on his face and seemed to
regard all the pageantry, and the honours of the day as nonsense, and fun. It seemed as though all these honours concerned any one rather than himself.

'At last the Duke began: "I want words to express—."'
The Prince Regent promptly interposed, "My dear fellow,
we know your *actions*, we will excuse your *words*, so sit
down." This the Duke did, with all the delight of a school-
boy who has been given an unexpected holiday! . . .

'. . . In the evening there was a ball; and the Duke of
Wellington danced a *polonaise*. Blücher joined in that, and
then danced a country dance in the German fashion, with an
allemand, skipping down the middle of the room with Lady
Burgersh. Old Platoff performed what he called a national
dance, with Miss Fitzroy. It consisted in stamping his feet
like a horse, and nodding his head. The whole thing was
exquisitely ludicrous, and the Duke could not help joining
in the general laughter. During the whole evening the Duke

was making jokes with his nieces, and appeared to enjoy the ball quite as much as they did.'[3]

In the meantime, the question of the Princess of Wales's income had come up before Parliament. Castlereagh wrote to say that he had been commissioned to propose an increase of £50,000 a year and that the amount of her debts was to be laid before the House. 'She received this intelligence without any manifestation of joy or surprise,' wrote Lady Campbell, 'and only said, "C'est mon droit,". . . However, that this news did give her considerable pleasure, I am sure.'[4] Whitbread, on the contrary, thought the offer 'insidious and unhandsome', but Caroline decided to ignore his protest. 'If de Princess refuse,' she said, 'dey will say—what de devil does de woman want? We cannot make her husband like her, or make de Queen receive her; but we can set de seal upon all our public doings of last year, by settling upon her a sufficient sum to enable her to hold de rank of Princess of Wales—a rank of which we tink her worthy, and wid her rank she must hold all her privileges. I will therefore accept —I will; and I will do it myself.' Lady Campbell thought she was right, 'especially as her enemies have always said that she threw herself into Mr Whitbread's protection entirely to make a disturbance.' Whitbread was surprised and mortified by her defiance and Lady Campbell said, 'I believe Mr Whitbread to be a most upright, kind hearted man; but he has the notion, which all Englishmen, nay, perhaps men of all countries, entertain, namely, that *men* only can act on the public stage of life.'[4]

Now that her financial worries looked like being happily settled and there was no further hope of recognition from the departed rulers of Europe, London ceased to hold attractions for Caroline. She rented a house and went down to Worthing for the summer season.

CHAPTER VII

The Jardin des Plantes and the Musée des Monuments

THE naval review at Portsmouth caused confusion along the whole of the south coast, as dozens of the packet boats that plied regularly between England and France abandoned their usual occupation and sailed off, with a load of sightseers, to join in the fun. The Reverend William Shepherd was one of those detained in Brighton, impatiently waiting at the Ship Inn for a passage to Dieppe. After a wait of twenty-four hours he was able to set sail with a motley group of males and females. Though it started in a gale, the little boat was soon becalmed in mid-channel in view of five Russian men-of-war steering from Portsmouth to the Strait of Dover. The passengers included an exiled priest and an angry Bonapartist, coming back from a stay in London. The latter had not enjoyed his visit. He found the Londoners rude, laughing at him for not knowing their language and mocking at his wife's tall hat. Shepherd paid two guineas for his berth, four times what Haydon and Wilkie had been asked for the same journey only a month before. The passengers were annoyed at having to pay three shillings for their passage in the little shallop which conveyed them from the stony beach to the packet.

It was Shepherd's second visit to the continent. He had been one of the many English who had taken advantage of the brief Peace of Amiens, and he was able to make interesting comparisons between the France of 1802 and the present day, especially the improvements made by the ex-Emperor. He had already been to the Louvre and was excited at the prospect of seeing the conqueror's additional spoils. An experienced traveller, he took along his own knife and fork. At Tôtes, the landlady of the posting inn tried hard to buy them from him but he would not be persuaded, promising to bring her some on his way back. France was suffering an acute shortage of steel and many people, he noticed, tried to buy knives and scissors from travellers. He had arranged to stay at the Hôtel de France in Rouen, but the driver of his cabriolet had other ideas. He appeared to have an understanding with the Hôtel de la Marine, for he took his passenger straight there, pretending it was the right place. When the clergyman protested, he was driven in a circle through the darkness and deposited at the back door of the same establishment. Shepherd spoke excellent French and was not to be fooled. After protracted arguments he was taken to his chosen destination. He was to regret his success before morning, for he got no sleep at all. A band played loud military music all night. The next day he discovered the culprit to be an English baronet, who, having no desire for rest, had combed Rouen for violin, horn and bassoon-players and paid them to entertain him through the hours of darkness while he sat in the dining-room drinking burgundy.

Shepherd made his way to Paris through Louviers and Mantes. 'Several troops of cavalry, which had constituted Wellington's army, were parading for a march to Gisors, on their route to Boulogne... Both men and horses looked remarkably well.' The children in the villages were so delighted to see any Englishman that they bombarded his carriage with roses and branches of flowering cherry. He had his first sight of Paris from the heights of Montmartre. 'On the evening of that ever-memorable 30th of March,' he reflected, 'this spot was crowded with people, who distinctly saw, with various and indescribable emotion, the battle which preceded the surrender.'[1]

The site of this day's fighting, when the Russian army had stood so near the gates of the capital, was one of the things visitors were most curious to see and the people of Montmartre earned a useful extra income taking tourists to the windmill on the heights or showing them round the church on whose spire the telegraph was fixed. 'From the top of a telegraph the country for many miles around may be viewed, while Paris, with its magnificent domes, and various public buildings, lays at the feet of the spectator. It is impossible to imagine a more diversified, extensive, and magnificent view.'[2] This optical telegraph was one of a network of similar devices placed on high points all over France at a distance of two or three leagues. It was the invention of the Abbé Claude Chappe and his brothers and their first line of communications had been set up between Paris and Lille in 1794. Each telegraph consisted of a tall mast, mounted either on a convenient church or on a tower specially built for the purpose, topped by a cross beam and two arms for signalling, worked by pulleys. The stations were manned by a watcher with a spy-glass who would read off the distant message to his companion, who, in his turn, started to re-transmit it to the next in line even before the sentence was finished. In this way, it was reckoned, news could reach Paris from the Mediterranean coast in less than fifteen minutes.

Henry Wansey surveyed the battlefield from the telegraph and was astonished to find no dead bodies or other signs of conflict in a place where so many lives had been lost. The Duke of Rutland went up later in the year and was given a vivid description of the action by the old soldier who had charge of it. 'From all accounts it appears that there was mismanagement on the Allied plans, and that they might

have gained their object at much less loss. Indeed it seems
certain, that there was a great useless sacrifice of lives on
both sides. The Allies lost 15,000 men for the purpose of
showing the Parisians they could fight; and the French lost
16,000, for the sake of proving that Paris was not abandoned
without a struggle.'[2] In spite of the recent carnage the land
looked in good heart, with the promise of a particularly fine
harvest if the weather, which was more settled in Paris than
in London, managed to hold. Indeed 'the crops of corn are,
if possible, more abundant and luxuriant than in any other
part. This is accounted for by the circumstance of its having
been a severe frost at the time of the battle. The horses and
men trampled the earth into a dust, which became such a
fine mould upon the arrival of a thaw and rain, that the seed
which was already in the ground came up with more than
ordinary vigour and luxuriance.'[2] Wilkie and Haydon dined
at a little public house on top of the hill and Wilkie made
sketches of the windmill and the church. Haydon managed
to find more evidence of devastation that Wansey had seen—
'houses absolutely bored with musket shot' at Belle Ville
and the Butte de Chaumont and several with 'their corners
and roofs beat in with cannot shot.'[3] At Pantin he saw 'a
beautiful house, furnished in an elegant manner, absolutely
reduced to a shell, to bare walls; in the parlour, horses had
been stabled, and their dung was yet on the marble floor.
All the windows and cupboard doors had been wrenched off
to burn; the paper of the rooms had been torn down; the
wainscot had been beaten in with the butt end of muskets
here and there, in order to see if valuables were concealed,
and the glasses shivered to atoms. Many of the fruit trees in
the garden had their stumps cut, and the garden itself, fitted
up to be sure in the French taste with statues of Shepherds
and Shepherdesses, was trampled on, and in a state of perfect
desolation. "Vous êtes Anglois, sans doute," said the shrewd

old Frenchman who showed me the house. "Oui," said I. "Ah, you fight for the *good* cause," said he, looking cunningly at the ruins about him. "Yes, I do," I answered, "But recollect," I told him, "that you have given Europe the same sort of proof of a *good* cause, and you amused yourself at Moscow, and now they amuse themselves here." "Ah, cela est vrai, Monsieur—la sorte de la Guerre. But," said he, "it is not the French people who have been guilty of such conduct but their Governors." "Then why do you suffer yourself to be duped by such Governors? I'll tell you what," said I, "if your Nation were a little more attentive and a little more interested about the conduct of your Governors, and took more interest in your national affairs and constitution, you would not be at the mercy of every rascal who choosed to struggle for the lead." "It is all true, Sir," he said, but I saw he hardly apprehended me." [3]

In Pantin 'the people were busy repairing, singing gaily, as if it were a good job, and we met many carts returning with beds and bedsteads and household furniture, which in the confusion had been carried into Paris . . . every crack and corner that was capable of defence bore the marks of murderous fighting.'[3]

Earlier the same day Haydon had paid a visit to the Château de Vincennes. This gloomy fortress was a magnet for the sort of tourist who enjoyed a macabre story, being the place where the Duc d'Enghien, son of the Prince de Condé, had been imprisoned and murdered. None of Napoleon's deeds had made so sinister an impression on English minds as the cold-blooded shooting of this young prince, on a false accusation of plotting against the regime, at dead of night in the castle moat beside a grave dug ready to receive him. It was the kind of setting that appealed to Haydon's over-vivid love of the dramatic. 'I felt exceedingly affected. There was something severely terrible in the look

of the Castle surrounded by a deep moat, a drawbridge, small
windows, grated, and an iron railing on the top for the
prisoners to walk inside, gave one an idea of the state of
tyranny, that nothing in England excites the slightest association of. How little do we know of such fear and apprehensions. The Governor was a fine, soldierly, polite fellow, who
had lost his leg at the battle of Wagram. He gave me permission to make a sketch of the tower, and afforded me every
convenience.'[3] Haydon asked a few questions, venturing as
far as he dared on the delicate subject of the Castle's recent
history. The replies were polite but evasive. He fared better
than later visitors. No doubt the importunate curiosity of
English visitors quickly became an embarrassment, for in
the autumn permission to see the moat or to make sketches
was generally withheld.

A more cheerful venue for tourists was the Jardin des
Plantes, not merely a botanical garden, as its name implied,
but a sizeable zoo, larger and better kept than any to be seen
in England. Haydon felt there were some remains 'of
Roman magnificence in suffering wild animals to wander
about at ease in spacious yards, without confinement or
restraint.'[3] Wilkie was particularly struck by the lions, 'they
were beyond everything',[4] and amused at the fact that one
of them kept a tame dog as a pet. John Scott, editor of *The
Champion*, counted six of them on his visit and remarked on
the same phenomenon—'One of the lions has a dog for his
companion, of whom he appears fond, smiling at his sport.
The dog keeps barking at the spectators, and the lion, retired
behind, looks on with the frank, and mild, yet noble air for
which this quadruped is remarkable. The dog appears to be
proud of serving him.'[5] The animals occupied about half the
extent of the gardens. There was a panther, a wolf of the
Ardennes, hyenas and a porcupine. 'Five bears, in three low
enclosures, surrounded by parapets, afford much amusement

to the spectators in the garden. Being young, they are pretty tame, and are easily prevailed upon to climb the trunks of trees, which are placed before their dens.' There was, besides, a large fierce bear who was famous for having killed his attendant. A visitor had dropped a five franc piece into its cage and the old soldier who looked after it had ventured in to collect the coin and had been hugged to death for his pains. Ever since then the bear had been called Martin after his victim, an example of French humour that shocked Wilkie profoundly—'instead of feeling horror, they think it a good joke.'⁴ Behind the enclosures 'range almost at liberty, the tamer quadrupeds, deer, gazelles, the strepsiceros, the elk, the white goats of Angora, several varieties of sheep, &c. Two camels are employed to turn the wheel of a forcing pump, which raises water to the gardens.'⁵ There was one elephant, 'young and without tusks, but bulky and in good health. He amuses himself within his enclosure by scattering dust over his body with his trunk, or by catching articles of food presented to him by his visitors.' Exotic birds roamed tamely round or swam on the ornamental water, 'and the most pleasant ideas are called up, on walking through these shady enclosures, and seeing the antelopes, and wild goats, and deer, and fowls, tame, and approaching to solicit food.'⁵

The Jardin des Plantes housed several buildings, the Cabinet d'Histoire Naturelle and the Cabinet d'Anatomie Comparée, where daily lectures were given on Botany, Vegetable Physiology, Anatomy and Zoology. M. Cuivier, the anatomist, was busy on a project to assist the study of evolution, assembling the skeletons of all known quadrupeds and birds, together with a complete series of the bones of each, separately labelled and arranged. The walls of his private cabinet were covered 'with wooden and pasteboard boxes, in which he assorts and names the bones which he is constantly receiving.'⁵ The largest public room contained the 'mummies and skeletons of the human species; among the least pleasant of sights.'[4] Haydon and Wilkie shuddered at the prize exhibit—the skeleton of the fanatic who had murdered General Kléber in Cairo in 1800 and had been impaled and subjected to various forms of torture. The curator allowed favoured visitors to shake hands with this grisly relic—'the bones of his right hand black from the burning.'[3] In another room wax models of fish and shellfish, 'constructed with the nicest art, and displaying the true colours', fascinated tourists who had seen nothing like them at home. 'Snails in wax are attached to real shells, and caterpillars to leaves and branches of trees. In one case the anatomy of an egg is displayed in twenty-four preparations, from the first appearance of the speck of life, to the chicken bursting from its shell.'[5]

The Musée des Monuments Français provided another curious attraction. This was a collection of tombs and memorials, rescued by a private citizen from the revolutionary atheism which had desecrated graveyards and turned churches into Temples of Reason. A few of the tombs actually contained the remains of the people they commemorated—'Molière, La Fontaine, Boileau',[5] for instance —but most, like the one carved with the recumbent figure of Henri IV, were empty, and the place was more like a museum than a burial ground. Wilkie thought it a 'very fine way of preserving' the monuments, 'they derive great effect from the order in which they are arranged, and from the decorations with which they are accompanied of old stained windows, &c. Perhaps the most interesting of all the monuments is that of Abélard and Héloïse, and this, in point of picturesque effect, is very beautifully placed in a garden, surrounded with trees, so disposed as to form a very pleasant background.'[4] Beside the lovers' tomb stood the ruins of the Chapel of the Paraclete, the oratory built for Abélard by his students at Nogent-sur-Seine. It had been removed from its original site and re-erected in Paris in 1802. Haydon observed that the monuments were not so defaced in France as they would have been in England, 'the people have evidently more feeling for this sort of thing.'³

If the Musée des Monuments lacked human interest for not housing many of the bones the tombs had originally covered, the Catacombs at the Barrière d'Enfer suffered from the opposite disadvantage;—'there are a vast quantity of bones in this place, but the catacombs had not the interest I expected,' Wilkie complained, 'and that arose from not having the means of knowing to whom the bones belonged. They appeared only an immense mass of the material of human existence, which had once formed part of the bodies, but which do not now characterise any quality of the minds to which they belonged.' Visitors were given a candle each to light their way down the narrow stairs; 'on coming to the bottom we were conducted through a number of passages cut out of the rock, till at last we came to the place where the bones are kept. This was a very singular sight. The walls seemed built with the bones of the human bodies, and at certain distances there were layers of skulls, which are placed in rows with a sort of uniformity, and even neatness, that with any other material would have been pleasing.'

Haydon was not much better pleased than his friend when he came upon some human remains that were startingly less removed from reality. 'As I was walking by the Seine on Sunday I went accidentally into a sort of open house, and to my surprise saw three dead bodies lying inside a sort of glass-house; here they lie till they are owned, as I found. Women and children, playing battledore on the other side, when the shuttlecock was down would quietly walk over and take a peep, and when they had satisfied their curiosity resume their game, repeating the process at intervals. I must own I never was so shocked—such palpable indifference and indecency. If this be not a way to use the people to blood I know of none more effectual.'[6]

Corpses, in this summer of peace, were being fished almost daily out of the Seine, prompting the papers to remark that suicide was becoming almost as much of a national habit in France as it had always been in England. For all Madame de Staël's complaints about tranquillity and boredom not everyone was at peace. Discontent was particularly noticeable in the army. There was a mutiny at Nemours and incidents began to be reported in the capital. Late in June two officers of dragoons created a minor riot by going into a bookshop that exhibited a collection of anti-Bonaparte pamphlets and scattering its stock to the winds. They spat on miniature engravings of 'Monsieur' and damned the whole race of Bourbons. The unfortunate woman who kept shop and 'whose crime of loyalty was thus visited on her means of living, had spirit enough to threaten them with a complaint to the police.'[7] They left, threatening to bring reinforcements to break her windows and turn her children into the street.

The Royal Family was working hard and unsuccessfully to earn the affection of their people. The Duc de Berri tried to emulate Napoleon, galloping fast and often through the streets and spending his days reviewing troops. The Duc d'Angoulême set off on a tour of the ports, while his wife thankfully left the gaieties of Paris to take the waters at Vichy. 'Monsieur' had been unwell and was confined to St Cloud, so that the palace had to be shut to sightseers. Since his rapturous reception in April his popularity had suffered a sharp decline, owing principally to his extreme conservatism. In July Louis had a severe attack of gout and had to hear mass in his private apartments. Shepherd, waiting to see him on his first public appearance after this illness, noticed that the cries of 'Vive le Roi' were few and lacked enthusiasm. The weather was mercilessly hot and dry, the river low, the people's tempers frayed. Now that peace had become a commonplace the Allies were fast losing their popularity. The crowd included some British soldiers in scarlet and Shepherd observed that they were stared at offensively.

Though the British might be jeered at in the street, nothing could exceed the courtesy with which they were received in private. Those who remembered French society before the Revolution noticed a radical change in the life of the upper classes. There were fewer private fortunes and life for the remaining rich was simpler and less showy. 'Once admitted into the family circles of the better class of gentry at the present day, you would admit that nothing can be more agreeable or amiable. Their manners are simpler than formerly and their characters more serious... What appears to an Englishman a subject for delightful interest, the relations of man and wife, and parent and child, approaches more nearly to our own notions of domestic happiness than we knew them about thirty years ago, or than they have since been described to us... Obnoxious and disliked as England is at the moment, for many reasons well known on this side of the water, nothing can exceed the obliging and friendly kindness with which we are individually treated by our French acquaintance; nor could anything justify the suppression of this tribute to private gratitude and friendship.'[7]

Sir Charles Stewart had returned to the Embassy after his visit to London for the reception of the Allied Sovereigns. He sent a note to William Shepherd's lodging inviting him to attend court to be presented to the King. Like other English visitors, Shepherd suffered from a valet-de-place who thought he knew everything. 'I was informed by our domestique,.. that as an ecclesiastic I had only to equip myself with shoe buckles, as shoe strings were not admitted.'[1]

Accordingly he drove to the Tuileries and was shown into a small room on the ground floor where he found Stewart and the representatives of Russia and Prussia. Stewart hastily came over to protest that he could not possibly be presented as he was with a coat 'en froc', Cursing his valet with un-clerical vehemence, Shepherd rushed to the Palais Royal, where he managed to get himself fitted up with the proper clothes and return in time. He was led up many staircases and through magnificent rooms to the presence chamber, where his Ambassador was waiting to introduce him. Louis came in, wearing the Cordon Bleu. 'He was uncomfortably corpulent, and seemed very infirm on his feet; but his countenance is extremely pleasing, and, if any reliance is to be placed on physionomy, he is a man of very benevolent disposition.'[1]

On the day Shepherd was presented to Louis, David Wilkie was posting towards Calais in the public Diligence, having left his friend Haydon behind him. He had stayed a month in Paris. He paid ten francs to the passport authorities for permission to travel, hopefully scattered copies of his prints in as many shops as would take them, and made a present of a small reticule to his amiable hostess Mme Lenoble as a reward for her attempts to teach him French. Haydon went to the neighbourhood of Notre Dame to see his coach off, and later confessed to his diary, 'My dear Wilkie set off this morning for England; in spite of Wilkie's heaviness of perception and total want of spirit as to gentle-manly feeling, his simplicity and honesty of manner, his good sense and natural taste endear one to him. I feel low at his departure, though I shall soon see him.'[3]

CHAPTER VIII

The Great Fair

PREPARATIONS for the Great Fair had been going
on throughout July in London's Royal Parks. *The Times*,
which deplored it as much as the Quakers, though for
different reasons, unwillingly printed an announcement of
the project, adding its own rider—'as other publications
have got the subjoined piece of nonsense, we are obliged to
insert it likewise. The public will first gape at the mummery,
then laugh at the authors of it, and lastly will grumble at the
expense. We are chiefly sorry, on account of the contemptible
light in which it will exhibit us as a people to foreign nations.
The Pagoda, the Balloons, the Girandoles of Rockets; the
Chinese Bridge, also—the Pons Asinorum; .... Alas! Alas!
to what are we sinking!'[1]

The Fair was in honour of Wellington, but the general
was not allowed to languish uncelebrated in the time between its announcement and its opening on August 1st. He
was feasted at Guildhall, where he was presented with a
sword of exquisite workmanship; given a ball at Burlington
House by the officers of the General Staff, and fêted by the
Regent in the illuminated gardens of Carlton House. Lady
Shelley was able to improve her acquaintance with her hero.
She gave a party for old Blücher, who, with Platoff, had
remained after the departure of the Sovereigns, and Mrs
Wellesley-Pole brought Wellington along to it. 'The Duke's

manner is formal, and, at first introduction, very imposing. He seldom speaks until he is well acquainted. He greeted Shelley with the utmost cordiality—having known him before he went to Spain.' Though Wellington had 'received honours enough to turn the brain of an ordinary great man, he retains the simplicity of character, and manner, which is still his distinguishing excellence. He remembers his old friends with the same interest as ever; and the youngest of his subordinate officers enjoys his society, and is indeed much more the object of his attention, than are those of a more exalted station in life. In the course of the evening, when I had lost something of the awe which the Duke's presence inspired, I ventured to converse with him. From that time our acquaintance increased, till it has almost become intimacy.' She invited him to dine on the day of the Prince's Fête and was delighted that he had come in full uniform, with all his decorations. We thus had the opportunity of examining the Spanish Order of the Golden Fleece. . . It is superb, being composed entirely of diamonds, suspended by a red ribbon. . . After dinner we all went to Carlton House, and I walked about with Wellington from supper time until we went away at 5. We watched the dancing for some time, and the Duke appeared to enjoy seeing all his a.d.cs dancing. He said: "How would society get on without all my boys?"'²

The streets continued to be thronged, crowds forming round any building where the hero of the moment was expected, or strolling in the parks to gaze at the progress of the Pagoda and the Chinese Bridge. Paris had been without rain for weeks, but England was suffering curious and changeable weather. In the last week of July extraordinary thunderstorms broke out with hailstones the size of hens' eggs and lightning so frequent as to provide almost continuous illumination. One boy was said to have been blinded by

a flash, and the village of Rearsby in Leicestershire claimed
it had suffered an earthquake. This state of affairs was not
propitious for Mr Sadler, the aeronaut, whose exploits were
to furnish the most notable entertainment of the Fair, rival-
ling Paris's intrepid Mme Garnerin. He had made a trial
run, early in July, ascending from Burlington House with
his seventeen-year-old son. *The Gentleman's Magazine* published his account of the flight.

'In a few minutes we were perpendicular with Leicester
Square, and our prospect was at once grand and awful; the
whole of London, and its magnificent buildings lay below
us, with its surrounding fields, canals, and parks; the beautiful serpentine form of the river, with its rich shipping, docks,
and bridges. We enjoyed this scenery for about fifteen
minutes, and, at a quarter before 4 o'clock, entered a dense
cloud, which completely shut us out from all sight of the
earth; at this time we could sensibly perceive the balloon to
be rising. When we had soared through this cloud, my son
observed to me, that, from the variegated colours reflected
and refracted from the multitudinous congregation of
vapours around us, and the effulgence of different lights, he
could scarcely see to any great distance, or make any distinct
observations on the numberless forms around us; although,
from the shadow of the Balloon on the more opaque clouds,
I could easily discover that we had already altered our course
towards the South East. From the intense cold, and a most
violent pain in my ears, which I never experienced before,
our height could not be less, in my calculation, than five
miles.' After a time the balloon came within sight of the sea,
and Mr Sadler decided it would be prudent to descend. His
son opened the valve and they began to go down rapidly.
'The clouds were so near the earth, that, after lowering for
the space of a quarter of an hour, though we distinctly heard
the lowing of cattle, we could not discover *terra firma*; but

shortly after the clouds opened themselves beneath us, and displayed the variegated fields and the river Thames. . . After again descending below the clouds, we saw an inviting hay-field at a considerable distance, and opening the valve again, a sufficient quantity of gas escaped for us to reach the pro-posed spot; and, after throwing out the grappling iron, which immediately took effect, we came to the ground with-out any unpleasant convulsion.'³ The two men collected their apparatus and were able to bring it back to London on a chaise hired in Brentwood.

On his next flight, Sadler took Miss Thompson as his passenger, a brave young lady who had already made one ascent with him from Dublin. For the opening of the Great Fair it was arranged that the Balloon should go up from the gardens of Buckingham House, taking Mr Sadler, junior, and 'a new aspirant to celestial excursions, Mrs Henry Johnson.'³

The first day of August dawned inauspiciously;—'the morning came; the sky was darkened, the rain descended in torrents, and the expected pleasure of the day was given up for the moment as lost.'³ By 11 a.m., however, the sun appeared, 'beaming in all his glory, and shedding his brightest refulgence on the scene.' Everybody started run-ning towards the parks, through streets where all the shops had put up shutters for the day. Some public buildings dis-played a little poster saying, 'Let not the people . . . listen to those who would poison their minds—to those who are the constant enemies of public joy', construed by *The Times* reporter as referring to his employers. The more elaborate pavilions were in Green Park, while Hyde Park was full of privately erected booths—'round, square, triangular, and polygonal, waving with the flags of all nations, . . . fabri-cated of those habiliments which once enjoyed other honours on the forms of female loveliness and manly virtue; delapi-dated petticoats, pantaloons with a single leg, old sheets glittering with the insignia of the Regent, and facsimilies of the physiognomy of the illustrious Wellington, covered the ground for many an acre.'[1]

The Queen and the Princesses, up from Windsor for the festivities, came out on the lawn of Buckingham House, anxious to examine the mechanism of the Great Balloon. It was then discovered that the fastening which secured the network to the valve had become disengaged so that it was held by a single string. After examining the damage, the Duke of Wellington managed to dissuade Mrs Johnson from getting into the cab. He did his best to dissuade young Mr Sadler also, but the aeronaut, 'feeling for the disappointment of the publick, and for his own honour' was adamant. He sailed off over Deptford, scattering little parachutes with patriotic tokens behind him, but immediately over Woolwich Wellington's fears proved justified, for the string broke 'and the main body of the Balloon was forced quickly through the aperture nearly eighteen feet. Mr Sadler, to prevent the danger which threatened him, caught the pipe at the bottom of the Balloon, and by hanging on to it and the valve line, he prevented the Balloon from further escaping. The valve, which had for some time resisted every attempt to open it, in consequence of being frozen, at this time gave way, and suffered the gas to escape. A sudden shift of wind, whilst the Balloon was apparently falling into the middle of the Thames at Sea Reach, carried about a hundred yards over the marshes on the Essex side, when the aeronaut seized the opportunity of making a gash in the Balloon with his knife, which the wind considerably widened, and occasioned the escape of gas in great quantity... Mr Sadler's descent on this account was rather more precipitate than he could have wished. He landed however in Mucking Marshes sixteen miles below Gravesend, on the Essex coast, without sustaining any other injury than a slight sprain.'[3]

The principal attraction of the Fair's first day was an elaborate battle fought on the Serpentine. Since Bony was no longer an interesting public enemy, one of the fleets hoisted American flags and was driven into shore, 'coming in stern first and firing one pop gun at a time',⁴ to patriotic cheering from the banks. Green Park was hung with Chinese lanterns, transparencies of Wellington and other heroes. Thames watermen had brought boats on to the canal and the public was permitted to take trips on 'this Regal stream', competing in races. Most people had become thoroughly weary before the climax of the day, when the great fortress erected in the royal gardens was transformed into the Temple of Concord. One by one the fortifications were removed as the building revolved on its axis, revealing a series of allegorical paintings—'The Delivery of Europe from Tyranny', 'The Restoration of the Bourbons by the Aid of the Allies', 'The Triumph of Great Britain under the Government of the Prince Regent', &c.

Most of the spectators agreed with the carping press that the illuminations were not up to recent standard, the Chinese lanterns too dim, the transparencies insignificant. Londoners had seen enough of such things for one summer. Some even complained that Mr Sadler's balloon was 'one of the meanest in device that we have ever seen' and 'destitute of the least ornament.'¹ The Press got their greatest satisfaction, in a spirit of 'I told you so', when the upper towers of the Pagoda burst into flame. At first everybody cheered what they took to be a rather more effective display of fireworks than any they had seen so far, but it was soon revealed, by the panicked cries of workmen, that the entertainment was not intended. Fire engines hurried to the scene and a man was discovered at the top of the tower, signalling in distress. Among the watching crowd was Mr Folkes, a bankrupt hosier who had already distinguished himself and earned a useful reward at a fire in the Custom House. He rushed again into the flames and was seen climbing towards the trapped man, but before he could reach him there was a loud explosion and he was forced to jump off, landing on a raft floating on the water. He was rushed to hospital, but was not expected to recover. The unfortunate workman perished.

The next day Londoners, disappointed by the Fair, had a new diversion offered them. A woman called Johanna Southcott announced that she was pregnant with the True Messiah and expected to be delivered of him in a few weeks. His cradle, presented by 'a woman of fortune', was being exhibited at a cabinet maker's in Aldersgate Street where it drew enormous crowds.

The month of August saw a second exodus from England. The first travellers, who had gone off immediately the Channel had become free, had now come back. They had consisted mostly of the middle classes, lawyers, clergymen and men of business. The new wave of travellers included members of the nobility, leaders of society and government officials who had delayed until after the visit of the Allied Sovereigns and the celebrations in honour of Wellington. The Duke and Duchess of Rutland had not waited for the Fair, but left from Brighton on July 29th, taking their carriage and horses. When the jubilee was over, a number of M.Ps sailed from Dover, with 'the wind blowing hard and the sea running high,'[1] to gain first hand impressions of the state of France. Lord Charlemont, the Marquis of Huntly and Lady Rolle had arrived in Paris, and Miss Planta, who had been a lady-in-waiting to the Queen with Fanny Burney, wrote to her friend that the capital was again half peopled by English. Madame de Staël's hopes were being fulfilled. The Earls of Romney and March, the Marquis of Bute, Lords Clanwilliam and Apsley left Dover for the continent. John Philip Kemble and his sister Mrs Siddons were off for a prolonged visit to the Paris theatres. Lord and Lady Castlereagh, with Lady Mary Stewart, began the journey that was to end at the Peace Congress in Vienna. Mr Astley, the London impresario, was in Paris trying to arrange an English theatre there. He had been to the Tuileries, where Louis decorated him with the Order of the Fleur de Lys.

Sir Charles Stewart also was going to Vienna, leaving the Embassy in Paris vacant. The Prince Regent decided to appoint Wellington to be his new ambassador there, and the Duke spent his last week in England in a whirl of festivity. His last engagement was a dinner with his regiment at Windsor. He came back to London to give away his niece, Emily Pole, at her marriage to Lord Fitzroy Somerset, arriving late at the church in a market cart, into which he had sprung, fully dressed for the ceremony, when the wheel came off his carriage in a street in Brentford. He set off for the continent on August 9th on a stormy sea, the Duchess following two days later. Meanwhile the Fair continued, causing annoyance to the private citizen and outbursts of moral indignation from the Press. Police were forced to raid the more blatant of the gambling booths in Hyde Park and *The Times* complained that 'the diversions of the lower orders have received daily encouragement from the visits of ladies of the higher ranks.'[1]

The Regent's birthday celebrations, on August 12th, saw London having its last, rather feeble, fling of this summer of rejoicings. Bells were rung, flags flew on St Martin-in-the-Fields and other churches and the Tower fired a salute of thirty-two guns. In the evening the parks began to fill with as many people as had been in them for the Fair, but the crowd was doomed to disappointment. There were no fireworks and the Sadlers did not go up in their balloon. After some hours, country people, who felt they had made a journey for nothing, decided to provide their own entertainment. They tore down the weather-soiled decorations of the Temple of Concord to make a bonfire of them. Spectators at a distance jumped to the conclusion that houses were burning and sent for the fire engines. Others tore down branches from trees in Green Park to improve the blaze. It was a melancholy end to the Grand Jubilee.

At Frogmore things were happier. Queen Charlotte entertained her son to the largest banquet she had given since her husband's illness, eating off gold plate among three hundred guests under two marquees that had once belonged to Tippoo Sahib. In Brighton, the Prince's favoured resort, sixty-five tables were laid on the cricket ground and, after the vicar had said grace, upwards of six thousand people were regaled with beef and pudding.

The last parties of the London season had been given and the capital fell into its usual summer quiet. Miss Berry went to Scotland for the hot weather; Lady Campbell to Worthing. The Princess of Wales had left that resort the day before her husband's birthday on the frigate *Jason* for the relative freedom of travel in Europe. Their daughter, Princess Charlotte, was going to Weymouth for the bathing. Lady Shelley, bereaved of her hero, retired to Maresfield, writing in her diary the day after his departure—'The adoration felt for the Duke by his family, his children, and, above all, the Duchess, are proofs of his greatness of heart, and disposition. He is undoubtedly the finest character that any age has produced.'[2]

Shortly after the Regent's birthday, his suite prepared for their summer holiday at the new pavilion in Brighton, sending ahead several waggon-loads of violins, 'cellos and clarinets from the band from Carlton House. Prinny himself arrived on August 19th and remained about two weeks. His stay was a sore disappointment to the town, which hardly knew that he had come or gone. 'As His Highness never showed himself in the town, his presence was only known through the medium of his attendants and friends, who sometimes condescended to lounge upon the Steyne. Lord Petersham and Lord Fife still parade the public walks; the former remarkable for wearing what is called the Prince's uniform, the latter for his introduction of a Spanish girl who dances with more agility than grace . . . the rest of the company consists of about one tenth of respectable merchants, and of nine tenths of utter nondescripts. Indeed, even when the Regent was here, the company was by no means of corresponding rank; a few Nobility were at the Pavilion, but scarcely any of the old families, who no doubt prefer their magnificent country seats to the salt air of Brighton. . . The town is a good deal crowded by persons on their way to and from France; no less than three packets left this coast for Dieppe yesterday.'[1]

It was said that in the last two weeks of August more than 1,200 new passports had been issued in London by the French Ambassador, almost exclusively to 'persons of the middle rank of society.'[1]

CHAPTER IX

The New English Ambassador

THE Duke and Duchess of Rutland arrived in Paris at midnight on July 29th and were mortified to discover that the rooms they expected to be waiting at the Hôtel Grange Battelière had never been booked. The place was full and they had to spend the night at an indifferent lodging house. They were shocked to find, in this capital of cookery, that all they could get to eat at so late an hour was half a cold fowl. The next day, by the good offices of Count Dillon, they were more comfortably settled and began a round of calls. On Sunday they attended Mass at the Tuileries, during which an hour's concert of music was played for Louis by the band from the Opera. They were shown over the state rooms of the palace and were astonished to see they all still held Napoleonic symbols, the letter N, the bee and the eagle, which the king had not taken the trouble to have removed. The Duke was introduced to the Marshals Marmont and Macdonald and was delighted at the tones of admiration in which they spoke of the 'talents, skill and modesty' of Wellington and their eulogies of the good conduct and regularity of the English troops, particularly on their march to embark from the northern ports. Calling at Peregaux, the Duke and Duchess were pleased to receive 328 gold Napoleons for £300, 'an evident symptom of the improvement of the state of exchange between the two countries, in favour of England.'[1]

The bees and the capital Ns bothered General d'Arblay, too. Their presence on the royal throne particularly embarrassed him on the day when, wearing the ugly uniform that offended Fanny, he stood on the king's left hand to watch the new Ambassador present his credentials. Louis replied to the Regent's message in a loud voice that the marshals and spectators in the hall could hear perfectly. He desired above all to see peace established on a secure foundation. 'For that I need the powerful co-operation of His Royal Highness. The choice he has made of you, sir, gives me hope. He honours me... I am proud to see that the first Ambassador England sends me should be the great Duke of Wellington.' 'As for the speech of the hero,' wrote d'Arblay to his Fanny, 'Even though I was as near as your bed is to your chimney-piece, I did not hear a word: he spoke so quietly and in a voice that almost trembled. I think I have already told you that we have an order from the King not to regard etiquette when it is a question of the English, who are admitted whenever and wherever they present themselves: but the manner in which he treats the man who represents them in indescribable. As soon as the Duke of Wellington appears, one is aware of the extreme satisfaction that is spread on all the details of the good King's face. I wish you could have witnessed, last night, the expressive face of the hero, who stood on the first step of the stage of the throne of which he seemed to be the principal support. He had a little the expression of saying, "I have in a small way contributed to its restablishment": but that with so modest an air that one could scarcely seize this fugitive idea... Nobody in the hall was better able to see or to examine him than your unworthy servant who was placed on the left of the throne, about in the same position as he filled on the right. I think he may well have envied me the pretty neighbours he could see near me, and who, in truth, I had a little assisted in their efforts to get there.'[2]

It had been evident for some time, as Shepherd had remarked in the crowd outside the Tuileries, that the people of Paris were in an increasingly discontented frame of mind. The euphoria that had filled them in welcoming their conquerors had vanished to the winds. British uniforms in the streets were no longer the object of amused curiosity. Whatever golden opinions the Marshals and the King himself might have expressed about the most illustrious wearer of them, it had hardly been a tactful move on England's part to appoint Napoleon's most successful military adversary to be her peaceful representative in the capital.

In the country, travellers noticed a growing reluctance on the part of the peasants to admit France had ever been conquered. The Emperor, they insisted, had been betrayed 'by his Marshals and the Legislative Assembly'.[3] The excessive number of troops permitted under the Peace Treaty threatened trouble if occupation was not found for them. 'The army, it is said, is disposed to go to war with anybody (perhaps with the exception of England); and even the court would not be averse to a partial and temporary war—which on the one hand would rid it of a tumultuous and troublesome guard, that may at last become a guard of janissaries, and, on the other, would have the effect of rendering the Duc de Berri popular with the army.'[3] It was thought wise for Britain to keep troops enough in the Netherlands to prevent a sudden *coup de main*. The Duke of Rutland heard the opinion of foreigners in Paris that Elba was an unwise place to keep Napoleon. It would be far too easy to call him back if war should break out on the continent.

The Duke of Wellington shared these apprehensions. Before settling down to his peaceful duty as British Ambassador he wanted to make sure that Belgium's frontier was well secured against invasion. Accordingly he had approached his new situation by way of that country, now incorporated

in a single kingdom with the Netherlands, and spent a fortnight 'riding round the Belgian villages with three Colonels
of Engineers.'⁴ He wrote his conclusions in a memorandum
which indicated good positions for an army at various points,
of which the last was 'the entrance to the Forêt des Soignies
by the highroad which leads to Brussels from Binch,
Charleroi, and Namur.'⁴ It was the ridge of Waterloo.

In the middle of the previous month the French Parliament—the Chambre des Députés—had been presented with
an Exposé of the cost to the country of the late war and of
the present financial position. Ten million pounds invested
in artillery and stores had been lost in the last campaign; the
funds of the army and navy showed a deficit of thirteen
millions. The matter which was being hotly debated in
August was the question of the freedom of the Press, one of
the Allies' original conditions for the restoration of the
Bourbons. Freedom was something French journalists had
never enjoyed and the argument was closely watched by
their counterparts across the Channel. In another matter the
French showed a more liberal spirit than the English, by
admitting ladies to the Chamber on the day the Budget was
read, 'a precedent which, perhaps, it will not hereafter be
found convenient to follow.'³ It was a precedent which, once
established, was hard to go back on. Shortly afterwards one
of the debates on the Press was brought to a total standstill
by a number of elegant women who stormed the doors and
overpowered the sentries when they were told that all the
public seats had been filled.

The weather had continued hot and sultry, the narrow
streets of Paris dirty and airless. Visitors with time and
money to spare took carriages and drove out into the country
round about, and, in particular, to the various royal palaces.
The Rutlands went first to St Cloud, leaving Paris by way of
Bonaparte's new Pont de Jéna, a light elegant bridge that

excited much admiration; past the Ecole Militaire and the Champs de Mars, 'rendered famous by the recollection of the fête, which was held there by a nation of infatuated idolaters, in honour of the Goddess of Reason.' They drove through the Bois de Boulogne, recently the site of Cossack encampments. The scenery was still beautiful, but most of the large trees had been cut down for the needs of war, leaving only the undergrowth and young saplings. The Palace of St Cloud stood on an elevation 'commanding a most beautiful view of Paris, with its various noble buildings... The river Seine forms a beautiful semicircular sweep below the esplanade.' This had been Napoleon's favourite residence and was at present the home of the Comte d'Artois. Haydon, who had not been able to see inside because 'Monsieur' was indisposed, was not surprised the Emperor had preferred to live on this airy eminence, surrounded by the finest trees in all France, rather than in Versailles. The palace was divided into different suites—the apartments of Napoleon; Josephine's wing, and the rooms specially decorated for her supplanter, the Austrian Marie-Louise. 'Besides these,' wrote the Duke of Rutland, 'there are the state rooms which have been so lately fitted up, that Bonaparte had only inhabited the palace fifteen days since their completion; a large salon, a gallery 120 feet long, and the chapel. The decorations throughout the palace are very magnificent; but we observed that those which are ancient have a decided superiority over the rest, which have been executed during the reign of Bonaparte.'[2] The Duke and Duchess were shown the library in which the late Emperor had passed most of his time, 'the floor of which (as we were informed by the domestic which officiated as our guide) was frequently strewn with maps, over which the plotter of mischief was wont to pore.' They saw the place where he had liked to eat his breakfast 'in the open air when the weather permitted, under the shade of a fine avenue.'[1] It was impossible, the Duke reflected, not to admire Napoleon, but 'his memory can never be encircled by that species of admiration which is paid to the actions of the virtuous and truly great. It will be said of him, when nothing remains but the recollection of his wonderful achievements—

> 'He left a name at which the world grew pale,
> To point a moral and adorn a tale.'[1]

From St Cloud it was a natural progression to Versailles, and most sightseers stopped at the village of Sèvres between the two palaces to look over the porcelain manufactory. At the August rate of exchange a complete dinner service made here cost about £250. There was a magnificent blue and gold vase on view, made to the order of Napoleon and valued at 30,000 francs, but English visitors were assured that it was not so fine as the one Louis had recently sent to the Prince Regent as an expression of gratitude for his sojourn in England.

It was even hotter when the Rutlands spent their day at Versailles. They went in a mixed party of French and English, with the Dillons and their daughter, Miss Ainslie, Miss Vyner, Mr and Mrs Heneage, M. Tuynot and his daughter and M. de Florigny, and ate a surprisingly excellent dinner in the inn adjoining the palace gardens, considering they had not ordered in advance. Versailles was always the most popular excursion outside Paris for the foreign visitor, with its dramatic associations with the Revolution. Those who had come in May and June had found the place in a sad state, 'very melancholy and overgrown with weeds, the roof letting in water.'[5] Haydon described 'painted ceilings faded! Crimson tapestries torn! golden freizes brown with age!'[6] By August 2,000 workmen were busy restoring the buildings to habitable order, a job that was expected to

take a year, after which Louis proposed to make it his
country residence.

Louis XVI's enormous château with its opera house stimu-
lated Haydon, who thought it must, in its glory, have been
'a gleaming jewel', to romantic flights of fancy. 'Invention
seems to have been ransacked to find excuses for new habita-
tions. I wonder they did not build a room for the King's
right hand and a room for his left, a room in short for every
action of his body and every conception of his mind. The
opera house was vast and melancholy, ruinous and dark.
Here Maria Antoinette sat on the night of her marriage,
young, lovely, and blushing! Here was assembled all that
was splendid, to bewilder her youthful senses, and left her
dreaming of uninterrupted happiness and undisputed
dominion. Her evil genius hovered over it all, and with
demoniac chuckle revelled at her approaching misery; had
she been endued with immortal acuteness, she would have
heard his devilish laugh, as the music died on the wind or
undulated on the waters.' He went with Wilkie to the
Grand Trianon, one of the many lesser buildings in the great
park, to look at the room which had been the study of 'the
disturber of the poor world's peace.'⁶ They looked with awe
at the candlesticks Bonaparte had used, the worn chair he
had sat in, the place his arm had rubbed on his desk, his
collection of military books. They penetrated into his bath-
room and imagined him lying in the water while his faithful
Mameluke, Rostan, stood guard at the door. They were disgusted by the formal outlay of the gardens.

Almost all English visitors reacted in the same way to Le
Nôtre's garden planning—the formal pattern of paths and
ponds and fountains; almost all of them were overcome with
sentimental delight at Marie Antoinette's so-called 'English'
garden at the Petit Trianon, observing 'a variety and beauty
that it is vain to look for in a French garden, the trees were

allowed to take their natural shapes, the pieces of water
followed the sweeps and turns of the ground in which they
lay, and the little walks were perpetually discovering to you
some new prospect, or losing themselves behind the rocks
or trees'.[7] Pursuing the winding walks, Wilkie and Haydon
came upon a collection of little cottages by the side of a small
lake, 'not much finer than might be seen in any country
village'. They were astonished to find, on going inside, that
they were full of splendid furniture. They had been built as
lodging houses for the dead queen's guests. 'The house of
Petit Trianon had been let out to a traiteur during the time
of the Revolution, and had received considerable damage
from the parties that used to frequent the house and garden.
But this seems now to be entirely repaired, and in such a
state as might convert even an admirer of Versailles to a
taste for English gardening.'[7]

The Duke of Rutland, more used than the middle class
traveller to the formal gardens of England's great houses,
differed from his countrymen in finding Le Nôtre's work
very fine indeed. He stood at a window in the upstairs gallery
of the palace and looked out beyond the 'fountains, and
waters, the bosquets, and groves' to a chain of hills on the
horizon covered with fine woods. 'We were particularly
fortunate in the moment at which we enjoyed this view, for
the declining sun was gilding with his last beams the fading
beauties of the scene, every feature of which partook of the
golden tint. One of the anterooms to the gallery, is the
Saloon of Peace, which formed one of the apartments of the
ill-fated Marie Antoinette, and it was here that she was wont
to receive her evening parties. Adjoining it was her bedroom,
in which we were shown the small door through which she
made her escape, naked and pursued, from the ponards of
the revolutionary murderers, who had previously slaughtered
at their post three of the faithful Swiss Guards, who stood at

The Allies visiting the brothel at No. 113 Palais Royal, Paris. By Opitz.

(*Radio Times Hulton Picture Library*)

The Great Fair of August 1814—the Chinese Pagoda and bridge in
St. James's Park and Mr. Sadler's balloon.

(*Radio Times Hulton Picture Library*)

François Joseph Talma as Hamlet.

the great door of the room.'[1] Darkness began to fall and the Duke and his party left, overcome with melancholy at the thoughts evoked by the great and derelict palace.

The King did not himself visit the Palace of Versailles till late in August, when he travelled down to examine the workmen's progress. It was said he bore the strain of the tour with perfect composure until they came to his sister-in-law's bedroom, when he burst into tears and sank on his knees in prayer.

Louis' coronation had been postponed. The day originally chosen had been the fête of St Louis, the day after Wellington's presentation at court. Instead, a splendid fête was announced to be given in the King's honour by the city of Paris. This turned out to be by no means so glorious as the papers of the next day, on both sides of the Channel, represented it—'the most trifling effects were extolled in pompous language.'[8] Salvoes of artillery were fired, there was a court at the Tuileries, 'and in the evening a concert to which admission was easily obtained by English gentlemen on their sending to the palace for tickets.' The theatres were open to the public gratis. One of these English gentlemen wrote to John Scott in some disgust, 'After reading the order of the minister of the police, for illuminating the front of every house, I expected a brilliant display, but I was disappointed. I repaired after the concert to the *Pont Royal*, as the spot where the superior blaze thrown on the elegant buildings which line the quays could be viewed to most advantage; but not a light appeared in the Louvre or in the Tuileries and its garden; single rows only graced the palaces of the Deputies and the Arts, and the gates of the Mint and hotels adjoining; but no greater lustre was thrown on the waters of the Seine by the whole illumination, than one sees on the Thames, when it is viewed from the Adelphi on a dark evening. A few boards hung with lights appeared before the gates of the

Luxemburg, and some hotels, but in most of the principal streets scarcely one was to be seen. However, next day every house in the city was described in the journals as having been illuminated from the first to the sixth floor. A good example of this people; they describe well, and ignorant of the comforts and the splendours of other nations, they feed their thoughts with their own vanity, and esteem Paris as the first city of the world, in spite of its wooden shoes, and its filthy streets. I could not perceive, on this occasion, a single glass lamp, or a transparency, or one instance of the public spirit of individuals; a few saucers of clay, filled with coarse tallow, and provided with thick wicks, form the only mode of illumination adopted here, exhaling a disagreeable odour, and having nearly the same appearance with the lamps in Clare and Leadenhall markets. Of the infinity of glass lamps, arranged in elegant devices, and sparkling with green, crimson, and topaz fires, to which the agitation of the air around communicates a waving effect, such as was often presented by Carlton House during the late rejoicings, they do not seem to have any conception.'[8]

Four days later Paris put on a more successful fête in its King's honour, and even this disgruntled Englishman had to admit it did not lack splendour. After Mass in the morning Louis received the Prefect of St Denis, who gave him a curious present—'a tablette, upon which were fixed two teeth of Henri IV, the whole of his moustachio, and some of the linen which had been wrapped round his body.' These grisly relics had been rescued from the church at St Denis at the time when the royal tombs had been desecrated during the Revolution. The King accepted the present with every symptom of satisfaction. The Duchesse d'Angoulême, back from her cure at Vichy, also received a deputation. Church wardens had made the long journey from Nîmes to tell her that their parishioners had made a solemn vow to dedicate

a silver statue of an infant to God if she would do the one
thing wanting to France's happiness—produce an heir of the
Bourbon stock. An English reporter was surprised at the
politeness with which she took this communication. 'Her
Royal Highness received it graciously, and even shed tears.
Elizabeth of England was always in a terrible passion
when any of her subjects talked to her about having an
heir.'³

Fountains ran with wine in the Champs Elysées from early
morning, and booths among the trees doled out provisions to
a good humoured crowd. The spectacle quite pleased John
Scott's critical friend, who 'met many of the lower orders
returning from the Champs Elysées, laden with eatables and
wine which had been scrambled for there; and as a Frenchman seldom shares in any pleasure in which his wife and
children do not partake, it was not unpleasing to view them
sitting down to the banquet thus provided at the doors of
their houses; a striking contrast to the solitary tippling of the
English peasantry. I witnessed no examples of intoxication,
though there were many enlivening cries of "Vive le Roi".'
He was pleased, too, with the good behaviour of a French
crowd. Private carriages were barred from the streets and
'the greatest order prevailed; for though robberies are not
unfrequent in Paris, pickpockets are rare, and indeed can
scarcely be said to exist. The intimate intermixture of soldiers
in every crowd or collection of people, however small, and
the consequent certainty of immediate detection, render
their profession extremely precarious, and prevent one from
feeling the same anxiety about pockets and watches, as when
surrounded by the London populace.'⁸ Later, crowds
assembled to watch Louis, Wellington, Talleyrand and
other notabilities drive to the state banquet at the Hôtel de
Ville. Early in the day the city sent to the palace to enquire
if the King, like Bonaparte, preferred to send his own cook

to prepare the dishes he would eat.' "My dear friends,"
replied the fat king, "tell the Municipal Body that when I
dine abroad, I bring nothing with me but a good appetite."[3]
It was remembered that the Emperor, when dining out,
brought his own food in covered boxes, to be heated up in
his presence by one of his own servants.

After dark the illuminations were, this time, nearly
worthy of the occasion, with a large star kindled on
Napoleon's Arc de Triomphe. In the Champs Elysées 'more
than thirty orchestras supplied dancers around them with
music; the walks were crowded with stalls of toys and
refreshments; jugglers, merry-andrews, and rope dancers
had been put in requisition: and a blaze of ten thousand
lights threw animation over the whole. No tree wanted its
lamp, and single and double rows of them were hung between all the trees in the principal avenues, the leaves of
which shone with soft and pleasing tints of green.' People
compared the cheerful festivities with 'the gloomy fêtes of
Bonaparte', but all was not as carefree as the Press would
have it. Early in the day there had been an acrimonious dispute between Louis' bodyguard and the National Guard, the
one claiming the right to be always at the King's side, the
other insisting that only they should have that privilege
once he was inside the Hôtel de Ville. 'Another question was
presented which was yet more perplexing: It had been
decided that thirty-six women should be admitted to the
royal table. But in what proportion should they be selected
for the municipal banquet from the new nobility, which
held their titles by terms of the charter, and the old nobility,
which had regained theirs? The new nobility was con-
founded when it saw that only five places were reserved for
it. The common citizens considered themselves still more
humiliated, since, among all the thirty-six ladies, there were
only two who did not belong to the nobility, and because at

a fête given by the city the municipal body was not represented by any woman.'[9]

The King went home to his palace by torchlight and his
arrival was the signal for the fireworks to begin. 'Rockets
and bombs ascended in quick succession; wheels revolved,
offering a variety of changes; a row of gerbes arranged on
the parapet threw their sparks into the Seine, and produced
the exact resemblance of a cataract of fire rolling down its
waves in succession; a temple in the centre of the bridge
shone out with the motto *A la Concorde*; and the expansion
of a large flight of rockets and the noise of an artificial vol-
cano, completed the scene. The whole was finished in a
quarter of an hour; and the crowd was just beginning to
move away, when Garnerin rose up slowly from the Eastern
side of the city, in a balloon. A circle of bright flames burnt
around his car, which were soon extinguished; but he continued to be visible for some time by the light of the full
moon. The crowd immediately separated and returned to
their homes; and by eleven the streets of Paris were as
deserted as they always are at that hour.'[8]

CHAPTER X

The Theatres of Paris

ON the morning of September 7th Paris had its first rain for many weeks and a number of visitors were deterred from going to the Champs de Mars to watch the King and his brother review the army. It was not only the weather that kept them away. Doctor William Roots, F.S.A. thought it would be 'the most critical day since the restoration'.[1] He had been warned not to go because, if trouble should break out, the English would be the first to suffer. Caricatures were much in vogue and French newspapers were full of them, the majority directed at the moment against English dress and manners. Anglomania was quite out of fashion, though the French seemed to dislike the Austrians even more. Later in the day the weather cleared and the sun came out as hot as ever, quickly drying the roads out of Paris. Several tourists decided to risk the review after all and, among their number, Mrs Siddons was observed, 'toiling along towards the Champs de Mars, heated and flushed, and in clouds of dust'.[2] An old accusation, that she was careful about her pennies, was brought up again. An alcove had been set up for the throne, in front of the Royal Military School, and an altar for the dedication of the colours. Louis made a brave speech, commending the army's zeal and effectiveness—'Let the enemy come when he will—but he will not come; we have none but friends!'[3] The Press reported shouts of 'Vive le

Roi', but Henry Crabb Robinson, among the crowd, thought they were few and fainthearted, except for the one or two isolated shouters whose voices quickly became familiar to anyone who frequented public gatherings in Paris.

Crabb Robinson was in the Grand Gallery at the Louvre some days later when he heard someone say, 'Mrs Siddons is below.' He abandoned the Titians and Raphaels to get a glimpse of her and confided to his diary, 'I am almost ashamed to confess that the sight of her gave me a delight beyond almost any I have received in Paris.' She was walking round the statues with the mother of Horace Twiss, and Robinson, who had never before been so near to her, followed as closely as he could without appearing to pry. In spite of his idolatry he noticed one or two small defects in his goddess. 'So glorious a head ought not to have been covered with a small chip hat. She knit her brows, too, on looking at the pictures, as if to assist a failing sight. But I recognised her fascinating smile with delight, though there was a line or two about her mouth which I thought coarse.'[4]

Sarah Siddons made her first visit to the Louvre in the company of Thomas Campbell, who later wrote her biography. They stood arm in arm gazing at the Apollo Belvedere, 'From the furthest end of the spacious room the god *seemed to look down like a president* on the chosen assembly of sculptured forms, and his glowing marble, unstained by time, appeared to my imagination as if he had stepped freshly from the sun. Every particular feeling of that hour is written indelibly on my memory. I remember entering the Louvre with the latent suspicion on my mind that a good deal of the rapture expressed at the sight of the superlative sculpture was exaggerated or affected; but as we passed through the passage of the hall, there was a Greek figure, I think that of Pericles, with a chlamys and helmet, which John Kemble desired me to notice, and *it instantly struck me*

with wonder at the gentlemanlike grace which art could
give to a human form with so simple a vesture. . . Engrossed
as I was with the Apollo, I could not forget the honour of
being before him in the company of so august a worshipper;
and it certainly increased my enjoyment to see the first interview between the paragon of art and that of nature. She was
evidently much struck, and remained a long time before the
statue, but, like a true admirer, was not loquacious. I remember, however, that she said, "What a great idea it gives us of
God, to think he had made a human being capable of
fashioning so divine a form!" When she walked round the
other sculptures, I observed that almost every eye in the hall
was fixed upon her, and followed her; yet I could observe
that she was not known, as I heard the spectators say, "Who
is she? Is she not an English woman?" At this time she was
in her 59th year; and yet her looks were so noble that she
made you proud of English beauty, even in the presence of
Grecian sculpture.'[2]

John Philip Kemble and his sister were staying in Paris in
an hotel next door to Talleyrand's house. Kemble had been
London's principal Hamlet for a good many years. In May
he had revived another play from his repertoire, 'Coriolanus',
and some critics had dared to suggest that he was getting too
old for the part. With Mrs Siddons, he was to be seen on
most nights in September in a box at the Théâtre Français
'paying great attention'[5] and John Mayne observed that he
was much pleased with a performance of Corneille's 'Cinna'.
Some English members of the audience hoped that he might
take back ideas for the improvement of their own theatre—
in the matter of costume, for instance. 'The actors and
actresses dress with strict regard to accuracy; the most indus-
trious investigations are made, with the assistance of the
learned members of the Institute, into the habits and manners of the period and people concerned in the play,—and on

this basis of truth its decorations are got up and its arrangements made. But not a thought is wasted on what is so
essential to the popularity of a representation in England,—
glitter, and show, and pomp. If they arise from a regard to
facts and proprieties, well and good;—if not, the audience
does not resent their omission. The hardware brilliance of
Mr Kemble's helmet and shield in Coriolanus would excite
the laughter and hooting of the judicious critics of Paris.'[6]

The classical austerity that prevailed in French drama, the
observation of the unities, the fact that there were rarely
more than two actors on the stage at a time, the plainness of
the scenery, the absence of a drop curtain or music between
the acts, bothered a nation brought up on Shakespeare. The
more thoughtful were impressed. 'The necessity of some of
these severities may be disputed, but it will not be denied
that they fairly try the sterlingness of the dramatic taste of
the people; and the result proves to be very superior to that
of the English at present, debauched as the latter has been
by the greedy and ignorant theatrical management, protected
in its folly and rapacity by an abused and unjust monopoly . . .
It surprises an Englishman to see this volatile people listening to long dull speeches, kept up between two performers,
with the regular alternation of a debate in Parliament, and
totally unrelieved by processions, by changes of scenery, or
even by brilliant costumes.'[6]

France's two national theatres were the Opéra and the
Théâtre Français. Unlike the legitimate theatres, the Opéra
went in for magnificent scenery and had an orchestra of
sixty with 'five pedal harps and a leader who stands up and
beats time to the performance.'[7] Visitors greatly admired the
ballets, performed by a company led by Vestris, and felt
there was nothing to be seen in London to compare with
them. The singing was another matter. The Duke of Rutland
thought it 'exceedingly despicable'[8]; the Reverend William

Roots likened it to 'the bellowing of bulls and the screeching of owls.'[1] A seat at the Opéra cost from 3.60 to 10 francs. At the Théâtre Français, which had the best actors, and showed the plays of Corneille, Voltaire, Racine and Molière, the prices ranged from 2.20 to 6 francs. The Opéra Buffa mounted Italian opera by Cimarosa, Paesiello, &c, and the Opéra Comique light French productions. The many legitimate theatres included the Théâtre de l'Impératrice, des Variétés, du Vaudeville, the last showing topical plays by contemporary authors.

The greatest attraction for visitors in the summer of 1814, especially for those whose French was not equal to the dramas of Corneille and Racine, was the 'translation' of 'Hamlet' by Ducis, starring France's greatest actor—Talma. London audiences were used to seeing their Shakespeare doctored by various adaptors, but even so most English were affronted by the liberties the Frenchman had taken with the story. Wilkie found this play 'so adapted as to produce a very striking effect upon a French audience. Talma played Hamlet, and in a scene which was nearly the same as the closet scene, he acted as if he saw the ghost, but without any figure to represent that personage. In a scene afterwards, he brings in the ashes of his father in an urn, which he weeps over very much, and when his mother comes in, requests her to embrace it also. A very singular effect was produced by her going up to touch it, and shrinking back with horror. . . Hamlet was a very different person from what Shakespeare had made him, and so was Ophelia.'[9] Wilkie and Haydon first saw the play in the little theatre at Versailles in June, when Talma was on tour, and, as usual, Haydon expressed himself more vehemently than his companion. 'Ophelia was murdered, and Hamlet literally rendered a blubbering boy. "Oh ma mère, mon père!" Ophelia is with Hamlet entreating by her affection to be more composed, when his Mother enters. Here, as he is talking, he sees the Ghost. The impression on the audience and the effect on me was certainly dreadful. I shall never forget it and it has shaken my orthodoxy as to the admission of the Ghost. It was truly terrific to see Talma's terrible look, and the stupefied amazement of his Mother and mistress. There was some cause for their amazement, when nothing was to be seen. Hamlet in the next scene brings out an urn that contains his Father's ashes. Here was the true French whine and affectation. Though when his Mother again returns, and he makes her swear she knew nothing of her husband's murder, and brings her to touch his sacred ashes, there was an awful silence and a severe agony throughout the house. The Translator has completely lost Shakespeare's exquisite feeling of "a grief within that passeth show" by making Hamlet's grief all show! and nothing else.'[10]

Their dissatisfaction with Talma's version did not prevent the painters going to see the play again when the great actor returned to the Théâtre Français. On this occasion a couple of Ducis' lines, inserted to please his countrymen, caused a nasty demonstration in the audience. When Claudius said—

> *'Laissons à l'Angleterre et son deuil et ses pleurs,*
> *L'Angleterre en forfaits trop souvent fut féconde.'*

the whole house burst forth in applause of the most tumultuous enthusiasm. 'This was mean and paltry, and was only the effusion of impotent malice for having been well beaten. It was the mouthing of a beaten boy who lies on the ground afraid to rise from the experience he has had of his adversary's strength. The people about us looked at us, but we were so high we did not hear distinctly what had been said. Had I heard it distinctly, I would certainly have said something. There was some row beneath us and I suspect from English men opposing.'[10]

In appearance Talma was 'by no means elegant or striking' and he adopted a style of acting favoured by all French tragedians, speaking in a high-flown and declamatory rhetoric. Most English visitors were won over by his genius, but he did not manage to convert them to French tragic acting in general. John Scott saw his Oedipus, 'and his acting in the scene where the horrible truths of his situation, after affrighting the wretched prince by indistinct shadows of misery and guilt, burst upon his knowledge as intolerable realities, was the most awful exhibition I have ever witnessed in public. We certainly have not an actor on the English stage that could have produced so prodigious an effect. Kean's bursts come the nearest to it, but they involve more of what seems peculiar to acting, and thus the spectator is relieved a little from the overpowering sense of distress: on the other hand, the indications of Talma's horror and agony, were dark, quiet, and simple,—illuminated only by an occasional glare of ferocity, which evidently belonged more to the man than to the part, and thus threw into the representation an assurance of reality, which it would otherwise have wanted.—On occasions like this, Talma drops entirely his false and strained manner, and then he appears the greatest actor of the present day. He had generally a touch of vulgarity in his acting, which often adds to its strength, and is much better than its artificialness.'[6]

The comedians of the Théâtre Français gave a more undiluted pleasure—the elderly character actor, Fleury, and the vivacious Mademoiselle Mars. All over the provinces, as well as in the capital, travellers remarked with wonder at the excellence of the small part players. 'Altogether,' wrote Ward to Miss Berry, 'the theatres are delightful. They really are a resource, which in London they are not. All within a stone's throw of the good part of the town, and of a size for hearing and seeing. Then too, the power of taking a box and keeping to oneself all the evening, makes an immense difference. I complain of nothing but their changing the piece after the boxes are taken, which is a downright cheat. For instance, everybody tonight expected to see "Le Misanthrope", which has been in the bills these three days, and this morning, without any reason assigned, they changed it to "Le Philosophe Malgré Lui." '[11]

Visitors' commendations threw as much light on the bad conditions of the London theatres as on the virtues of the French ones. Everybody was astonished at the quiet good behaviour of the audiences, for demonstrations like the one Haydon and Wilkie had witnessed were rare. 'The business of the stage is conducted with praiseworthy discretion, and confident reliance on the true dramatic feelings of the audience. There is no half-price at any of these places of amusement: there are no accommodations for prostitution let out by the managers: they do not share the profession and profits of those who keep the brothels of the Palais Royal:— their business is the drama, and to its performance they confine themselves. Thus their houses are not larger than sufficient to supply the legitimate demand of the public for this species of entertainment, and they permit each person who pays for admission, to derive the stipulated enjoyment of hearing and seeing.'[6]

The English were to provide the French with a new species of entertainment in late September, when Colonel Thornton sent for his hounds and led them through the streets of Rouen to the delighted astonishment of a thousand spectators. The Duke of Wellington sent for the pack he had hunted in Spain and was to be seen on the fine autumn mornings riding in the Bois de Boulogne with the Duc de Berri and other members of the French Royal family, followed by bevies of English ladies in open carriages. The new ambassador was busy looking at houses, seeking a new home for the British Diplomatic Mission, and was rumoured to be buying the Borghese Palace and the Château de Villiers, which had been the home of Joachim Murat, King of Naples. He had more serious matters to consider, his support having been enlisted in the question of the Slave Trade by Clarkson of the British Abolitionist party. He had some private conversation in August with Talleyrand, who expressed himself sympathetically on the subject, but he was less successful with the King. Louis repeated his anxiety to do all he could to implement the clauses of the Peace Treaty, but, as far as slavery was concerned, said he would have to go slowly. He reminded Wellington that it had taken a long time to convince the English that its abolition was desirable and nobody should imagine that the French could be converted in a shorter time. The Legislative Body and the House of Peers were dead against that particular clause of the Treaty. Ships were even now being fitted out at Nantes and Bordeaux, some with the assistance of British capital, ready to resume the trade along the coast of Africa. Above all things France needed to expand her commerce. Nothing could make Britain more unpopular than any attempt to interfere with it. Madame de Staël told Crabb Robinson, over a private dinner at her château at Clichy, that she sympathised with the aims of Wilberforce, but she did not believe the abolitionists had any chance of success in France.

The representatives of the allied nations were now converging on Vienna. On September 15th Talleyrand set out from Paris to plead the cause of his conquered country at the Peace Congress there. Crabb Robinson caught sight of him before he left, driving by in his carriage, and decided he had 'the countenance of a voluptuary or a courtier, rather than a politician or a man of business'.[4] There was certainly nothing of the man of God in the appearance of the ex-priest. He was observed to speak arrogantly to his coachman. From the waist down this man, with the glittering basilisk eye, seemed a sorry figure, with his thin legs and his deformed foot. William Roots, who went on a pilgrimage to look at the hotel where Mrs Siddons was staying, had a more informal view of the great politician. He saw him at the window of his house next door, 'practising his speech for the Congress of Vienna on his balcony in a robe de chambre'.[1] It was the day before he set out on his journey.

William Roots had arrived in Paris at the beginning of the month, one of the last wave of tourists before the autumn set in and the weather made travel increasingly difficult. France can hardly have been visited by a more alert and amiable representative of the English middle classes than this physician from Kingston, Surrey. He set out from home with his wife, his children, William Sudlow and Joney, and capacious notebooks and colourboxes for recording his impressions in prose and in paint. For the whole of his fortnight's holiday he kept scrupulous account of every penny or franc he spent in the inns of England and France and in the shops of Canterbury, Calais and Paris.

Roots must have been a tall man, to judge by his most frequently voiced complaint, that French beds were too short. In Boulogne he found them damp as well. His opinion of them was in sharp contrast to John Mayne's. Mayne had now gone on to tour the provinces, where he pronounced the beds to be 'clean and excellent (as usual)' and notably free from bugs and fleas. Paris was full when the Roots family arrived and they took some time to find a suitable lodging. The next morning, being a Sunday, the doctor took them to Mass at Notre Dame, where they heard 'an excellent sermon by the Archbishop of Paris.'[1] When they came out it was to find most of the shops open. Louis' edict, so enthusiastically obeyed on June 12th, had been more or less forgotten already, and the only appearance left of its being the sabbath, apart from the masses, was that the women in the streets were better dressed than on a week day.

Having consulted with Mr Philips of Peregaux and other compatriots met in that 'club' for visiting Britishers, on the proper way to live when in Paris, Roots set about hiring a valet-de-place and a private carriage. The latter was 'a mark of respectability'[1] and cost a louis a day. It was to give the little family intense satisfaction. Everywhere they went in it it was assumed they were members of the nobility and Roots was universally addressed as 'Milor'. Joseph, their valet, was a more mixed blessing. An ardent Bonapartist, he harangued the little party on politics, laying all the blame for France's defeat and the return of the Bourbons at the door of Marie-Louise. If only Napoleon had stuck to Josephine, he protested, he would never have been so silly as to go to Moscow and would still be enjoying the throne. Like so many English, the Roots family missed their roast beef and deplored the French mania for turning everything into fricassées and ragouts, but the physician was unusually adventurous with food. He was prepared to try everything once, even including a dish of frogs. On this occasion he could not persuade the other three to join him, for 'Joney noticed their little feet and screamed'. He persevered himself, though he confessed that he had to take a draught of brandy to keep them down. He considered the wine poor, but the brandy beautiful and mellow. He had a brave try at French beer, which he ordered to accompany prawns and lobsters, but pronounced it 'infernal stuff... resembling treacle and water made sour by standing and some tincture of quassia put into it.'[1] The little family felt themselves at the centre of high life, fetching their letters from the Embassy where they arrived in the Duke of Wellington's diplomatic bag; seeing the Kembles and the Marquis of Buckingham; let into Mass in the Chapel Royal, where 'poor

Louis waddled in . . . and bowed to the English bonnets.'[1]
They did all the proper things—watching the artists copying
pictures in the Louvre; looking at the bear 'Martin' and
shaking hands with the skeleton of Kléber's murderer;
visiting the Phantasmagoria, the Sèvres factory, the Tivoli
gardens, where they thought the China asters were planted
with too much regularity; Versailles and the Trianon, and
the scene of d'Enghien's murder. Under the golden dome of
the Invalides, the asylum for old soldiers, they endured
abusive remarks from the inmates with excellent humour,
'It would have been the same if Frenchmen had visited
Chelsea'.[1] Roots was particular, however, not to take his
wife and Joney to the Palais Royal—'The only place in Paris
where I think modest women should not go.'[1] But he did
not mind exposing himself and his young son to the
temptations of the place. He and Sudlow went there twice to
look at the gambling and to buy fairings in the little shops.

CHAPTER XI

'Monsieur le Duc de Vilain-ton'

THOUGH the papers reported 60,000 English in Paris on September 22nd, there was no doubt that travellers had begun an exodus, returning to the comfort and safety of their own country before winter set in and made the roads and the Channel even less comfortable than they were in summer.

'No man can take a sudden resolution to quit Paris,' wrote John Mayne, 'a permit from the proper authorities is requisite.'[1] William Roots collected his from the police in mid-September and on to Peregaux to draw enough cash to pay his hotel bill. Always fascinated by money, he had had the prudence to bring a sufficient supply of golden guineas, which got a better rate of exchange than letters of credit. His foresight gained him, he calculated, about eighteenpence in each guinea.

Most of the travellers who overloaded the packetboats at Calais and Dieppe in the early autumn went home grousing and grumbling, in striking contrast to the satisfied tourists of May and June. Prices had rocketed. The welcoming manners of the newly-defeated French had given place to a very different behaviour. Travellers were no longer a welcome novelty. Largely through their own foolishness, they had declined into a mere source of revenue. At Magny the Roots family, carrying their principal purchase, a French angora cat in a cage, stopped before an advertisement for the Hôtel du Grand Cerf before deciding where to put up for the night. Scrawled in an English hand on the placard they read—'Countrymen, this Hôtel du Grand Cerf is the most extravagant and filthy in all France, and I advise you to avoid it.'² They took the unknown's advice and spent the night at the Hôtel du Bras d'Or.

Another traveller, leaving Strasbourg for Germany, felt relieved to put France behind him. He had found it 'a scene of imposition to travellers. The people on the roads are as distinct a race as possible to that which we have been induced to think them. There is no longer "Milord Anglois" or "Oui, Monsieur". They are a surly, brutal discontented set. When they charge you (which they always do) more than four times the proper sum, and you pay it without a murmur, they regret they had not charged you more, and if you remonstrate with them on the exorbitance of the charge, they seem equally dissatisfied. We should have been plundered more than we were, if we had not latterly told the landlords that we were determined to insert their charges in the newspapers, as a caution to English and other travellers... I have lived at the Clarendon at one half the expense I lived at in small country inns in France. As to the beautiful filles de chambre which Sterne wrote about, he wrote from fancy, or the race is extinct. Now usually a raw-boned two-handed creature without shoe or stocking, before you have been out of bed half an hour, pays you a visit to ask for money.'³ It was to mitigate complaints of this sort that the French government made a decree that ordered every inn to keep an open book, from that September, in which guests could record their complaints against waiters, porters or post boys—or, presumably, against extortions on the part of the landlord.

It is fair to say that it was not only on the French side that

travellers were fleeced. At Dover and Brighton the little
boats that landed passengers from the packets were putting
up their charges. On one occasion at Dover returning tourists
refused to pay five shillings each and stayed on board until
another boat came out which offered to take them ashore for
three. The oarsmen in the first boat waited till they had
climbed on board their rival and then proceded to sink it.

It is also fair to say that though travellers complained of
French extortions they rarely made accusations of dishonesty
against their one-time enemies. The honesty of the French
countrypeople made many an Englishman reflect ruefully
on the inferiority of his own nationals in this respect. Crabb
Robinson and his friend John Thelwall had an experience
that was typical of many incidents recorded by visitors. They
had looked over the castle of Vincennes and then taken
dinner in a restaurant nearby. On their way back to Paris
Thelwall put his hand in his pocket and found he had come
away without his purse, containing 20 napoleons—about
£20. He recollected taking it out to pay the bill. 'We all
returned with him to the hotel; the house was shut. On
knocking, a chamber window was opened, and we heard a
female voice exclaim, "Ah, ce sont Messieurs les Anglais,
pour la bourse!" The maid and her mistress came down
together; and the former, who had found the purse on the
table, had it in her hand, with an expression of great joy at
being able to restore it; and she received Thelwall's present
very becomingly.'⁴

A good many of the travellers who, through nervousness
or the overcrowding of the Diligences, had come in private
conveyances at greater expense, plucked up courage and
made their way home in a cheaper manner. Wilkie and
Haydon, who had reached Paris in a hired cabriolet, had
left again by public transport, and most of their compatriots
did the same. On the whole they agreed that the government-

run French posting was better than the private enterprise
stagecoaches of their own country. Unlike the English
coaches, the French ones carried no passengers on the roof.
The inside held seven or eight persons 'very commodiously'.
'Outside three sat in front in a sort of one-horse chaise stuck
up against it'.[5] At the back was a similar arrangement in
which three men could sit, travelling backwards. The gentlemen descended and walked up the hills around Rouen and
Dieppe to ease the horses. 'The sound of the whip is forever
assaulting our ears,' wrote Wansey, but he went on to explain that the postillions were in fact very merciful to their
beasts. 'They seldom strike them, for the crack of the whip
keeps the horses on the alert, and they get on very fast.'[5] The
postillion in his enormous leather boots, the pigtail of his
old fashioned wig flapping against his coat collar, rode one
of the four horses, the other three being harnessed abreast in
front of him. His payment was rigorously controlled, and
published for the customer's guidance in a government book.
It was wise to be provided with the latest edition, for few
postillions were above trying to wangle extra money out of
the inexperienced on the plea 'que vous avez été superieure-
ment mené' or 'qu'il faut nous donner à boire'. Payment
was by the post, each horse being charged 35 sous between
every stage on the journey, with 30 sous for the postillion
and an extra charge, called Poste Royale, on entering or
leaving Rouen or Paris.

Mrs Siddons and her brother left Paris towards the end of
September, having disappointed patriotic hopes that they
would show off English acting there. The Parisians, no
doubt, were too well satisfied with their own excellent actors
to have thought to invite them. They went home by way of
Brussels and here John Kemble and his wife joined the
English players at the Park Theatre in a performance of
'Hamlet' that astonished an audience who knew the play

only in Ducis' mutilated version. Its verdict was not entirely
in Shakespeare's favour. The long speeches of the Ghost
bored them and they were shocked by the intrusion of the
Grave-diggers' comedy on the solemn drama. Kemble's 'fine
tragic talents' were admired, but 'the last scene of this piece,
however, which is eminently tragical, was in some degree
disturbed by a singular accident, a large bat made its way
into the theatre, and by its ill-omened presence alarmed the
ladies who filled the boxes; this bird of darkness flew about
everywhere, and even carried its irreverence so far as to settle
on the heads of the actors who were at that moment expiring
on the stage.'³ Its intervention 'gave to the Prince of Den-
mark an air of gaiety a little misplaced.'³

Though the tourists were leaving, there were many British
settling down for a winter in Paris for purposes of business
or of state and the streets were still said to swarm with them.
Fanny d'Arblay arrived at last to join her husband, having
been away from the country of her adoption since 1812,
when she had gone to England with their young son
Alexandre to avoid his being conscripted by Napoleon. The
French papers made an unfortunate gaffe by reporting the
presence of the Princess of Wales in their capital. The lady
in question turned out not to be Caroline, but Maria Fitz-
herbert, Prinny's morganatically married wife. The real
princess was by now well on in her travels, which took her
to Switzerland and Italy and to the Neapolitan court of
King Joachim Murat. Here she was to be seen, attended by
plump cherubs, riding in a shell-shaped golden carriage,
ridiculously dressed—'a fat woman of 50 years of age, short,
plump and high coloured' in 'a pale pink hat with 7 or 8
pink feathers, floating in the wind'⁶ and a white skirt that
hardly covered her inelegant knees.

Since the initial enthusiasm of Louis' return to Paris,
when a number of Bonapartist monuments had been hastily

taken down, the work of clearing away mementos of his rule had been virtually abandoned. Foreign visitors were delighted that most of the pillaged works of art still remained in the Louvre for them to gaze on, while in the Place du Carousel the Venetian bronze horses still stood on the unfinished Arc de Triomphe. No doubt the Congress, now assembled in Vienna, would be giving precise directions about their fate. In the meanwhile Paris was happy to keep them. In October, however, workmen began to dismantle the colossal statue of Dessaix in the Square des Victoires, to make room for a monument to the Happy Restoration. A reform even more fundamental to the life of Paris was now suggested. The Duc and Duchesse d'Orleans requested that the gamblers and women of pleasure should be expelled from their old residence, the Palais Royal. London papers were not approving. 'We respect the nature of this request, but doubt not a little of its policy. Great and luxurious capitals will be stained with vices; and when we look at the nightly state of our streets from one end of London to the other, we shall almost be inclined to envy Paris a building to which much of her dissipation and debauchery is in a great measure confined.'³

The hot dry weather of the summer had continued into late autumn and even in December the Seine was running so low that it was impossible to use it for commerce. It was barely deep enough to swallow the continued stream of would-be suicides. The difficulty of transport sent prices soaring and wood was now so expensive that the Parisians were forced to burn seacoal, which they detested. The price of wine had almost doubled, though it was still cheap by English standards. Mr Brackenbury came over from London in late November to negotiate for claret and carried away the entire output from Château Margaux and half of that from La Tour and La Fitte for the year 1812, said to be the best in living memory. The King was doing his best, out of a depleted revenue, to assist those who had stayed loyal to the Bourbons during their exile, but this did not endear him to the new nobility, many of whom still felt slighted since the civic banquet of St Louis' day. He tried hard to earn popularity, going to the public theatre once a week instead of having the actors brought to the Tuileries, appearing to the people as often as the state of his legs allowed. But the spectacle of a fat man in an easy chair could not hope to efface for long the image of a conquering emperor such as the people had been accustomed to. Monsieur had gone on a protracted tour of the provinces. The Royal Dukes were continually reviewing troops at the Champs de Mars to give them the illusion of activity, but John Cam Hobhouse heard that the Duc de Berri was hated by the soldiers, for all his efforts to win their loyalty. He had a violent temper and had been seen to strike an officer, and even, once, a common soldier on parade. The army was so tired of its life of in-action that when a mock battle was staged in a meadow at Clichy the troops lost their heads and attacked each other with real violence and hundreds had to be dragged off the field to be treated for cuts and bruises.

The Duchess of Wellington had come to Paris early in October, bringing the boys with her. She arrived to a cloud of rumours surrounding her husband, most of which linked his name with that of the opera singer, Grassini. He had met her in England, when she had been singing at Covent Garden at the time of the visit of the Allied Sovereigns. The Press reported her to be a frequent visitor to the Wellingtons' Paris residence—'Though her peculiar talents do not lie in the way of diplomacy, they ought at least to produce harmony between the British Ambassador and the French people.' Madame de Staël, who had invited the Duke to Clichy once or twice in June, before her visit to Switzerland, had failed to fascinate him, but he was known to dislike clever women. Now that she was back they met again, only to quarrel over the war in America. Their dispute, at a ball, reached the sedate columns of *The Times*. 'Mme de Staël ... has lately returned and resides within a mile or two of Paris, where her salon has become, as heretofore, the central point of the literary, political and fashionable world. It would appear that she had taken under her protection the United States as well as the house of Bourbon; for lately, on hearing of the capture of Washington she pronounced an oration in favour of that government which, as it happened to be in the presence of our Ambassador, seemed to be a challenge to His Grace, to prove that the sword is not his only weapon. The Duke of Wellington did all that Bonaparte himself could not do—he silenced her.'[3]

The American war, early in October, gave the French Press ample opportunity for being offensive to England and for stirring up the people into an anti-British frenzy. Disappointment with the Bourbons had already inclined them to turn against the country they had previously hailed as their deliverer and fears that England would enforce the provisions of the Treaty relating to the Slave Trade and spoil their chances to reopen commerce made her more unpopular still. A small and vociferous party of American diplomats and journalists were working successfully on Parisian feelings. The burning of Washington, described in France as one of the finest cities in the world, in England as a collection of flimsy buildings which had no existence twenty years before, was seized on by the Paris Press as a pretext to inflame the people. English residents were pelted with rubbish and insulted in the streets. The British general across the Atlantic was likened to Napoleon. 'Was it intended to furnish *Him* with an excuse, who was justly charged with trampling under foot all those principles, by imitating his

barbarous example? What! The English who reproached
him with such force and justice, with spreading pillage and
conflagration . . . with ruining and destroying the towns that
submitted to his armies, now make themselves masters of
Washington, plunder and lay it waste, blow up all its public
establishments and public edifices, and carry off in their
ships all that they do not choose to destroy by fire and sword!
It is not a foreign city . . . it is a city which may be called
English, which speaks the same language, which has the
same manners, and is composed of inhabitants whose fathers
were English!'³ Not for the first time in history Britain was
accused of hypocrisy; her excessive tenderness for the negroes
was contrasted with her brutality towards her own kith and
kin and interpreted as a jealous determination to prevent
France from enjoying the reopening of trade with her legitimate colonies. The French Press took leave to wonder why
England did not send Wellington to deal with the American
rebels instead of allowing him to idle his time away in the
drawing-rooms of Paris. The Duke, hunting his pack in the
forest of Rambouillet with the Duc d'Angoulême, had his
own excellent reasons for preferring to remain in Europe.
At the end of October, however, his brother-in-law, Edward
Pakenham, who had been his adjutant-general in the Penin-
sula, was sent across the Atlantic to take command from
General Ross.

No matter what the London papers might pretend to the
contrary nobody was less popular in Paris than the British
Ambassador. 'His nod,' said Hobhouse, 'is insupportable.'⁷
'Monsieur le Duc de Vilain-ton', he had been re-named by
Maréchale Berthier, when he arrived at a party in her house
late and insufficiently well dressed, having come from a hunt
in the Bois. She had not been amused, but the incident was
taken by some young men as an excuse to adopt a new informal manner of dress in the evenings in imitation of the

English hero. From mid-November there were almost daily statements, followed by almost daily denials, of his government's intention to recall him. It was recognized that his appointment had been a blunder. *The Times* voiced the people's anxiety on his behalf. 'The general opinion of the public respecting the Duke of Wellington's embassy will, we have reason to suppose, be verified by his Grace's recall. His life is even said to be in danger in the French capital, from the evil passions which his presence there has excited; and the most ordinary civilities or proposals are received with coldness and caution, only because they come from him. These representations are probably too strongly coloured; but still it is a matter of regret that the mischief, be its magnitude what it may, should not have been foreseen, rather than experienced. It would, indeed, have required infinite temper and address, at once to subdue and calm all the jealousies, envies and antipathies, to which a long course of opposition in the field had given birth.'[3]

The problem was how to withdraw the Duke without making him look foolish. The Regent was in favour of sending him at once to take command in America and Lord Liverpool was inclined to agree. Wellington refused their suggestion. He knew very well that his presence was essential to the safety of England. 'In case of the occurrence of anything in Europe, there is nobody but myself in whom either yourselves or the country, or your Allies would feel confidence.'[8] He had little liking for his position in Paris, but he did not want to be thought a coward. 'I confess I don't see the necessity for being in a hurry... I really don't like the way in which I am going away... I don't like to be frightened away.'[8] Eventually a solution was found that the Ambassador was prepared to accept. Lord Castlereagh was leaving Vienna to return to parliamentary duties in London and the Duke agreed to replace him at the Congress. He remained in Paris with his family for Christmas. On the day following news was brought to him by a courier from Ghent that peace had been signed there between Great Britain and America. The French were delighted. The end of the war meant the lifting of the British blockade on American ports and the prospect of improving their commerce.

Meanwhile it had been reported from the island of Elba that the work going forward to improve Napoleon's castle there had been suspended as long ago as September. 'This is not the only circumstance which induces an opinion that the stay of this famous personage on this island will not be long.'³

CHAPTER XII

The Long Cold Winter

THE removal of Bonaparte from Elba would, everyone now assumed, be one of the results of the Congress's deliberations. Most people felt his position to be dangerously near the coast of France, but they seemed more afraid of the moral effect of his proximity on the mood of the French than of any prospect of his leaving the island of his own accord. Not many people, on either side of the Channel, semed to be losing any sleep over the latter possibility. The London papers reprinted a French effusion on the extraordinary wisdom and virtue of the monarchs who were conferring in Austria or had sent their representatives and who would infallibly keep Europe safe from the menace of the Corsican ogre—Alexander, the Blessed; the intrepid Frederick-William; the self-sacrificing Francis, and 'the Prince Regent of England, who combines with the intelligence of the Monarchs most renowned for their prudence, the splendour of all the virtues of chivalry.'[1]

Ever since September these sagacious kings or their representatives, attended by a vast staff and a concourse of elegant ladies, had been indulging in the largest and longest party in history—theatrical entertainments and masked balls; hunting and shooting and staging mock mediaeval tournaments; decorating each other with orders and the colonelcies of each other's regiments; and, occasionally, finding time to meet over the conference table. It is recorded, however, that during the whole six months the Congress lasted the representatives of the Allied Nations never once managed all to sit down together.

The unpopularity of the English in Paris was in no way reflected in relations between the countries' two governments. Talleyrand, the defeated nation's principal representative in Vienna, was pro-British by inclination and had been working hand in glove with Castlereagh while the other victorious leaders danced or disputed. His motive was to split the Allies by supporting Britain and Austria against Russia and Prussia. Castlereagh disliked and distrusted Alexander and saw a way to keep the continental powers weak by allying himself to the subtle Frenchman and the ultra-conservative Metternich. Before he was recalled and replaced by the Duke of Wellington, he and Metternich had put their names to Talleyrand's masterpiece—the secret Anglo-Franco-Austrian treaty of alliance of January 3, 1815.

Though Londoners were able to take a personal interest in the activities of the Congress, having had so many opportunities in the summer to get to know the principal actors, Vienna was a long way off. The first excitements of peace had grown stale. During the autumn, while travellers came home from discovering France, people grew bored with politics and more domestic problems occupied their minds. They had heard enough of parties, fairs and festivals. When the Temple of Concord in the park was put up for sale, its decorations somewhat spoiled by weather, nobody could be found to bid for it outright. It was split up and auctioned piecemeal to a crowd that included few of the ordinary public and even fewer bidders. A posse of 'brokers, jobbing carpenters, dealers in old iron, copper, tin and canvas' from Moorfields and Seven Dials put in slow and unenthusiastic offers for a hundred small items. Some of the canvases—

'Strife Descending' and 'The Emperor Rescued'—went for
as little as eight shillings, though 'The Golden Age Restored'
and 'The Regent and Wellington' were fairly sharply con-
tested and made over three guineas each. 'Seven beautiful
vestals with vases of sacred oil, were disposed of for thirty
shillings or two guineas each, the purchasers undertaking to
carry them away at their own expense.'[1]

Few members of the public could afford to purchase
frivolous mementoes of the celebrations with the price of
bread now up to $1/1\frac{1}{4}$ the quartern loaf. Others, perhaps,
thought it not worth while to lumber themselves with
wordly goods when Doomsday was so short a time away. A
respectable farmer had already been ruined because he
believed Johanna Southcott's prophecy of the end of the
world and had not bothered to plant any crops for the year.
Unsuperstitious people blamed the papers for giving publicity to Johanna's pretensions. 'The more this imposture is
brought forward, particularly in respectable papers, .. the
greater attention does it excite, till at length many weak
persons, whose hearts are better than their understandings,
begin to wonder and become credulous.'[1] Some doctors
really thought the elderly prophetess was pregnant, but the
celebrated accoucheur, Dr John Sims, was sure she was not,
though he had no doubt that she was sincere in her belief
that she was.

Some of those who had not been ruined by their belief in
Mrs Southcott and could still afford to buy bread were now
considering the desirability of installing the new gaslight,
that had caused so much comment at the Peace Celebrations,
in their own houses. The idea sparked off an exchange of
letters in *The Times*. A gentleman calling himself by the
popular pseudonym 'Civis' warned of the grave consequences if a gas flame should accidentally be blown out. 'I
know not how it is proposed to guard against such accidents

in the employment of gas light *indoors*; nor do I believe it is possible to do so effectually, till a remedy is found for ignorance and carelessness in servants.'[1] He was promptly answered by one 'Gabriel Gas Light' who ridiculed the idea that gas could possibly explode even if a naked flame were taken into a room full of the stuff. Besides, he declared confidently, the smell would be so noticeable that nobody would dream of going near a place into which any had escaped. Before winter set in a number of the shops along Fleet Street were fitted up inside with the new source of light.

Tourists back from the continent were finding London much inferior to Paris from the point of view of the scholar and sightseer. They were shocked and ashamed to find the British Museum closed during August and September, just the moment when the capital was full of foreign visitors. The difficulty an alien had in getting into the British Museum Library at this or at any time was unfavourably compared with the courtesy and absence of red tape encountered by visitors requiring similar facilities in France. At least the British Museum did not charge for admission, if and when it was open, but Westminster Abbey, the Tower, the Monument and other places of note were blamed for making 'indecent extortions'. In Paris everything of the kind was free. No Englishman, besides, on being approached in the street, was ever able to give directions how to get to any place, whereas every French boy could conduct you to the Louvre. Travellers concluded that the French deserved their works of art, however they might have come by some of them, but that England had well and truly earned Napoleon's epithet—'La Nation Boutiquière'.

The French, again, deserved their excellent theatres. There were complaints that London managements were parsimonious. If one star in each production was sufficient to fill the house, they thought it wasteful to employ two. Thus the

The English family in Paris—a caricature after Carle Vernet.

Le Départ de la Diligence.

Louis XVIII fleeing from Paris in March 1815. From a nineteenth-century engraving.

principal actors, Kean and Kemble, were never seen on the
stage with the ladies who would have given them worthy
support—Mrs Siddons and her young Irish rival, Miss
O'Neill. As for payment, Kean was able only to earn £20 a
week in London, when he could get £100 a performance in
the provinces. London's theatreland had, besides, been dead
throughout the summer, an artistic drought not suffered by
the public in Paris. In September Covent Garden reopened
with Sheridan's 'Pizarro' and a set of new decorations dismissed by first night audiences as 'drab and dingy'. The
much advertised improvements amounted to little more than
a new canvas drop curtain of a muddy colour, dotted over
with splotches of a darker hue, presumed to represent roses.
A week later Drury Lane followed suit and was more highly
praised. The new decor was light and elegant and the work
of the summer months had included the removal of a number of pillars which had previously obstructed the view. The
play was again by Sheridan—'The Rivals'—but none of the
critics had room to mention so insignificant a detail of
the evening's entertainment. All their space was given over
to the new appearance of the theatre and to the special pro-
logue spoken by Mrs Edwin, a verse effusion on the subjects
of the recent war, trade, the lateness of the harvest and the
problems of slavery. A wit in the gallery earned himself
publicity at the expense of the actors by exploding firecrackers.

John Philip Kemble's first play after his months abroad
was 'Coriolanus'. The Covent Garden audience welcomed
him back vociferously and threw laurels on the stage at his
feet. At the rival theatre Kean was making his first London
appearance as Macbeth. He had been called 'the English
Talma', not only for his flashing eyes and his gift for tragic
roles, but from his short stature. He was twenty-five. It was
less than a year since he had made his first appearance in the

role of Shylock, an unknown actor from the provinces, to a
house less than half full. Now the theatre was crowded, the
pit enraptured, and laurels, this time plaited into a wreath,
thrown at his feet—a trick some people deplored as borrowed
from the French.

John Cam Hobhouse had met Kean in the summer at
Holland House, eating 'most pertinaciously with his knife'
and 'a little too frequent with ladyships and lordships'. He
described him as a little man in a pepper-and-salt suit,
'strongly made and wide shouldered, hollow, sallow face,
thick black hair.' Kean told him that he sometimes found
his voice to fail him on the stage. It had been described as
harsh and husky, but Hobhouse thought he had 'a sweet
accent and manner in private.[2] Keen had recently acquired
a horse, wondering whether he were not being a trifle pre-
sumptuous in thus assuming the habits of a gentleman about
town. The Sunday before the first night of 'Macbeth' he had
reason to be glad of the animal. He was returning home on
it over Hounslow Heath when he was set on by two footpads
who attempted to stop him. 'One presented a pistol and
demanded his money. Mr Kean immediately struck spurs to
his horse, who set forward immediately with such force as to
knock the fellow down, and strike the pistol out of his hand.
The other fired after Mr Kean but happily missed him.'[1]

By Christmas London's two principal theatres were staging rival productions of 'Macbeth'. Critics were now, evidently, prepared to take a leaf out of Ducis' book in the
matter of stage apparitions, for they were surprised, when
Kemble's version was revived at Covent Garden, that 'the
gross and improbable' spectre of Banquo was still permitted
to appear. Kean's production retained the Hecate scene,
which was praised for being 'almost poetic in its arrangement'.[1] Early in the new year the rival actors, the old and
the young, could also be compared in the role of Hamlet.

French actors had not yet penetrated as far as London, but in Brighton and other south coast resorts companies from across the Channel could occasionally be seen. They were not of the highest quality, and caused some people to wonder whether John Bull really wanted to see plays in French. From his education 'Greek or Latin plays would be more suitable and better liked than Molière.'[2] Brighton had continued popular and on fine days in late September crowds estimated to amount to 4,000 people paraded on the Steyne in carriages of every kind, from the barouche to the donkey-curricle. There were complaints about indecent sights on the beach, where people bathed from machines that were insufficiently screened from public gaze. 'A mere awning ... would effect all that seems necessary. Let not Brighton, which piques itself on its superiority, be outdone in decorum by Margate or Southend.'[1] By early October the crowds had thinned and the prices were coming down. The result, in the opinion of many, was to improve the quality of the society. 'Many widows and maiden ladies come for motives of economy. They come at the end of the season when there is more chance of being noted.'[1] The Queen herself chose to visit her son's new seaside pavilion after the crowds had dwindled. Prinny took her and his sisters for a walk on the Steyne on a warm day late in October, but even at that date they did not escape being followed by an immense crowd. The royal ladies stayed four days by the sea and then returned to Windsor, exchanging purses for posies with old and patriotic persons at every stop along the route. Alone among the princesses, Prinny's daughter, Charlotte, did not visit the new royal resort. She remained in her peaceful refuge at Weymouth until December.

Christmas was cold, and the royal family at Windsor were hardly able to venture out at all. To make up for the dry summer rain had fallen in cascades and the river that flowed past the royal residence was abnormally high. When the Christmas snow began to thaw the rising Thames waters rushed into the cellars at Eton to a depth of three feet. The first official bulletin of 1815 declared 'The King's disorder continues unabated, but His Majesty passed the last month in a tranquil state.'

It was in the new year that a notable event in London's musical life took place. On certain evenings of the week the principal theatres turned themselves into concert halls and early in February Drury Lane advertised, in a programme including choruses from Handel, Bach and Stevenson, the first English performance of 'The grand instrumental piece, composed by the celebrated Beethoven, in commemoration of the Battle of Vittoria, the manuscript score of which he sent to this country as a present to the Prince Regent.'[1]

'The celebrated Beethoven' had been, for a time, an ardent admirer of Bonaparte and had dedicated his third symphony to the Emperor, but his hero's subsequent conduct had changed his opinion and he had erased the dedication from the score. Beethoven was in Vienna at the time of the Congress and was introduced to the Russian Empress by the Tzar's ambassador there, Count Razoumovsky, whose name he was to make immortal by his quartets. The Battle Symphony was given, 'to the most unbounded applause', as part of the lavish entertainments of the Congress, two large halls being given up to its first performance. By his dedication of the score to the Prince Regent the impoverished composer was hoping to receive a useful sum of money from England.

London first heard the work, the worst, though initially the most successful, that Beethoven had ever written, on February 10th, when it was conducted by Sir George Smart before an audience keyed up to the pitch of expectancy. The orchestra had been augmented to nearly 200 performers. The critics were confused by the work but declared it to have 'the usual merits of the German school, great science, great depth of harmony, and, if that be a merit, great difficulty.'[1] The piece opened with the marching of the British army to the music of Rule Britannia, after which was heard a fanfare from the French army. English listeners questioned the accuracy of this. 'The composer must decide whether it is from English courtesy, or from a remaining prejudice in honour of his late master, that he has made the French challenge first. The commencement of the battle puts an end to all ceremonials and for the next ten minutes nothing is heard but the "regular confusion mixed" of drums and trumpets, violin and horn, in fearful imitation of musketry, the bayonet clash, the discharge of cannon, and the cries of the dying... Some of the contrivances to express the change of battle are curious,—the trumpets echo behind the stage to mark the decline of the French force,—and *Marlbrouk*, played in a *minor* key,.. is presumed to leave no doubt of the broken spirits of the piper, who has thus lost the power of blowing in tune.'[1] The Symphony included the tunes 'God Save the King' and 'For he's a jolly good fellow', and these, far more than the quality of the composition, provoked rapturous applause and a series of encores. The critics were tepid, finding that 'as a work of mere musical composition the piece has such excellence as belongs to Beethoven's style', but complaining that the composer had been unambitious in his depiction of battle noises, 'we in particular observed no attempt at the movements of cavalry'. There was no doubt, however, that no noisier piece had ever assaulted the ears of European concert-goers. 'Its animation and novelty,' predicted the critics, 'will, however, probably make it a favourite.'[1] They were right. By March 1st, by permission of the Regent, the Battle Symphony had been repeated six times.

The music critic of *The Times* turned out a better prophet, at any rate of the immediate future, than the popular Johanna Southcott. Excitement had risen, among a certain section of the public, as the time of her confinement drew near. This ought to have been mid-October, but by Christmas there was still no sign of the promised Shiloh or Messiah. Suspicions that a trick might be played on the credulous were increased when two men were arrested in Crewkerne, Dorset, for attempting to buy a baby from a woman who had been brought to bed of twins. Johanna's effigy was paraded in the streets by the angry people of the town. Nevertheless her followers were reckoned in thousands. She had claimed to be the 'woman clothed with the sun' from the 12th chapter of Revelations, and since her coming to London she had been busy sealing the elect for the next world at a fee between 12/- and a guinea. Three days after Christmas she was reported to have died, but the curious were prevented from dissecting her body to investigate the truth of her pregnancy because her followers were confident she would rise again within four days. Her body was kept warm with hot water bottles while crowds of her disciples prayed outside her house in Manchester Street. This treatment only accelerated nature's work and in a short time it became only too apparent that 'the wretched Johanna was but mortal.'[1] The doctors were permitted to move in. No Messiah was discovered in the elderly phophetess's womb. 'Thus finished a delusion which would have disgraced the most barbarous times,'[1] triumphed the scientifically minded. Their delight was premature. Johanna left no baby, but she had bequeathed a sealed box to her followers and her death by no means put an end to the curious religion she had founded.

The year 1814 had began in a war that had come, almost, to seem a permanent way of life, and which closed in a peace which seemed equally permanent. '1814,' said the leading article of *The Times*, 'will rank among the most remarkable in history. It has seen the downfall of the most formidable despotism that ever threatened the security of the civilised world. It has witnessed the restoration of a paternal government to the country which for five and twenty years passed through the greatest variety of conflicting revolutions. It has beheld all the Sovereigns of Europe assembled, personally, or by their representatives, *in peace*, to lay the foundations of permanent tranquillity, and to construct anew the social edifice, by the proportions of equity and moderation.'

CHAPTER XIII

The Eagles Return to Paris

THE Duke of Wellington took his leave of Louis in a long private audience on January 23rd, and the King gave him, as a parting token, a magnificent dinner service of Sèvres porcelain. Wellington left his Duchess in Paris, and Lord Fitzroy Somerset, who had married his niece Emily Pole, remained to act for him until another ambassador should be appointed.

The new year had come in to a series of splendid balls and receptions, given by the various royal dukes. The pleasure of the one given by the Duc d'Orleans was marred by the death of the attractive Princesse de Léon, who was burned alive when the crêpe of her gown caught in a candle flame while she was dressing for the party—a type of accident all too frequent at the time. Though the King was not as popular as he had hoped to be, his appearance in public still aroused loyal demonstrations from a people who enjoyed nothing so much as an opportunity to show emotion. When an English visitor was heard to object that the King had kept the theatre audience waiting half an hour, he was rebuked by an elderly Frenchman—'Sir, you have little to complain of. We have waited for him for twenty years.' At the opera 'Castor and Pollux' the entire audience rose to its feet and cheered Louis on the lines,

'The universe demanded thy return.
Reign o'er thy faithful people.'

The royal family had a more sombre duty to perform in
the grey and icy January weather. The mortal remains of the
guillotined Louis XVI and Marie Antoinette had been found
and exhumed from the lime in which the coffins had been
buried. It was said that the Queen's severed head was still
recognizable and there were fragments of dress to assist in
her identification. Louis' body had been reduced to bare
bones. 'Monsieur' and the royal dukes attended the exhuma-
tion, and the reburial at St Denis took place on January 21st,
twenty-one years, to the day, since the late King's execution.
The remnants of his brother and sister-in-law's clothing, in
particular a pair of elastic garters in a good state of preserva-
tion, were presented to Louis XVIII. The Sieur Descloseaux,
who, with his family, had guarded the secret of the burial
place, was rewarded with the Cordon of the Order of St
Michael and a pension for life.

On the day of the funeral the roads to St Denis were
covered with frozen snow. Clouds kept the day dark and a
minute gun sounded. The drums and trumpets were muffled.
All France was in mourning and the theatres closed. All the
way to St Denis the streets were lined with people, soberly
dressed and more serious and respectable than the English
correspondents had ever seen them. The murdered King's
two brothers and the royal cousins and nephews followed
the coffins, but, as was the custom, the Duchesse
d'Angoulême remained in the Tuileries, weeping and pray-
ing for her parents' souls. There was one sinister incident.
The decorations of the funeral car caught momentarily on a
street lamp at one point along the route and 'several people
set up the regicidal cry, the cry of the most terrible days
of the Revolution'—'A la lanterne!'[1] Some Frenchmen

considered the ceremony ill advised, but Madame de Staël reflected that it gave rise to so many demonstrations of affectionate loyalty that no blame could be attached to those who had planned it.

It would be unfair to suggest that the Duchesse d'Angoulême preferred funerals to balls and theatres, but certainly Marie Antoinette's daughter had little taste for the gay life of the court that winter. She was not, however, too serious to enjoy light reading, and had recently attempted a translation of Fanny d'Arblay's latest novel, the unsuccessful and generally more or less unreadable 'The Wanderer'. Hearing this, Fanny sent her the work in English, in a cherished copy which had belonged to her father, Dr Burney. Fanny had suffered pricks of conscience about the Duchesse ever since March of the previous year, when Lady Crewe had taken her to the wrong reception and she had been introduced instead to Louis XVIII. Her one-time mistress, Queen Charlotte, urged her to take steps, as soon as she got to Paris, to be presented to the royal lady. General d'Arblay was not rich and Fanny did not want to incur the expense of going to a public drawing-room, so the Vicomte d'Agoult promised to arrange a private audience. The Duchesse, for her part, was impatient to meet the well known authoress.

Fanny's husband took her to the Tuileries on an afternoon towards the end of February, but she was not allowed to enjoy his support for long. They were separated almost immediately and the shy and trembling Englishwoman was conducted through various anterooms, in each of which she was handed over to a different lady-in-waiting. Eventually she was taken into a largish apartment in which yet another lady was standing. By this time she was so apprehensive that she could barely reply to the formal civilities. She allowed herself to be seated beside the lady, but hardly listened to what was being said to her, for her attention was riveted on the door through which she expected to be summoned into the royal presence. It was only the egotism natural to an author that made her turn round, when her companion made a remark about her writing. 'I am quite sorry to have read your charming last work in French.'[2]

She turned now and looked properly at the lady, who went on to say, 'Puis-je le garder, le livre que vous m'avez envoyé?'[2]

'Startled, as if awakened from a dream,' wrote Fanny, 'I fixed her, and perceived the same figure I had seen at the salon. I now felt sure I was already in the royal presence of the Duchesse d'Angoulême, with whom I had seated myself almost *cheek-by-jowl*, without the smallest suspicion of my situation.'[2] Fanny was thunderstruck by this discovery, but quickly decided that it would be more tactless to admit her error than to behave as if it had never happened. She feared 'that Son Altesse Royale might be seriously hurt, that nothing in her demeanour had announced her rank; and such a discovery might lead to increased distance and reserve in her future conduct that could not but be prejudicial to her popularity, which was already injured by an opinion extremely unjust, but very generally spread, of her haughtiness. It was better, therefore, to be quiet, and to let her suppose that embarrassment, and English awkwardness and *mauvaise honte*, had occasioned my unaccountable manners.'[2]

From that moment the interview went beautifully. Too late to retreat into the proper formality for conversing with royalty, of never speaking except in reply to a question, Fanny chattered on, forgetting her shyness as she had in London at her meeting with the King; introducing subjects of her own. She told the Duchesse about her ten years' residence in Paris at the time when the French royal family had been in exile in England. There was one awkward moment, when the Duchesse asked how she had obtained permission to leave for England when the two countries were at war. Fanny had got her passport from a person whose name she could not pronounce in the hearing of a Bourbon—'Savary, Duc de Rovigo, whose history with respect to the murdered Duc d'Enghien has, since that period, been variously related.... I found, however, to my great relief, that the Duchesse possessed the same noble delicacy that renders all private intercourse with my own exemplary princesses as safe for others as it is honourable to myself; for she suffered me to pass by the names of my assistants, when I said they were friends who exerted themselves for me in consideration of my heavy grief, in an absence of ten years from a father whom I had left at the advanced age of seventy-five; joined to my terror lest my son should remain till he attained the period of the conscription, and be necessarily drawn into the military service of Bonaparte.'[2]

Soon after this Fanny recollected the Duchesse's long residence in England and exclaimed 'But why should I speak French when your Royal Highness knows English so well?'

'"Oh, no!" she cried, shaking her head, "very bad!"'

'From that time, however, I spoke in my own tongue, and saw myself perfectly understood, though these two little words were the only English ones she uttered herself, replying always in French.'[2]

The two ladies parted only because the Duchesse was summoned to the King's dinner table. She took her leave of Fanny with many messages of affection to Queen Charlotte and the Princesses. 'I little thought,' reflected the Englishwoman years afterwards, 'that this, my first, would prove also my last, meeting with the exemplary princess, whose worth, courage, fortitude, and piety are universally acknowledged, but whose powers of pleasing seem little known...'[2]

Two or three days later, on February 27th, the Duchesse d'Angoulême and her husband set out for Bordeaux, where they planned to remain for several weeks. She left Paris and its dissipations with no regret, though the journey, which took several days, involved her in the usual round of public appearances, the now familiar crowd of white-clad young ladies turning out to escort and serenade her at Orleans, Bourges and Limoges, where she stayed on the way to her final destination.

Wellington had reached Vienna, where the papers at once published alarming reports that he had fallen ill of a nervous disorder. Castlereagh was on his way home from the Congress, stopping in Paris to give Louis news of its deliberations. Amongst other matters, he had to inform him of the decision to retain Joachim Murat on the throne of Naples, at which Louis' usually amiable countenance turned purple with rage and he burst out with a half-stifled oath. Rumour suggested that Sir Charles Stewart, Castlereagh's half-brother, who had been the first ambassador in Paris after Napoleon's abdication, might be sent back to fill Wellington's place. Parisians refused to believe this on the grounds that he was not eminent enough to succeed the Duke; that another soldier would be most unwelcome, and that his having made himself notoriously unpopular with the Austrian Emperor was no good reason for sending him to France.

On the afternoon of Sunday, March 5th, Ignace Chappe, the corpulent director of the telegraph system, and brother of its Inventor, the Abbé Claude, rushed, out of breath and agitated, into the office of the Baron de Vitrolles, Secretaire des Conseils du Roi. In his hand he held a sealed dispatch. When he had sufficiently recovered to speak he refused to explain himself, but begged de Vitrolles to take the envelope, the contents of which had come over his brother's invention, immediately to the King. Louis was in his apartments, suffering from an attack of his usual gout, the disorder having affected his hands so badly that he had difficulty in breaking the seals. After he had digested the contents of the paper for some moments, his head bowed in his hands, he spoke to the Baron.

'"Do you know what this telegraph contains?"

"No, Sir, I do not."

"Well, I will tell you. It is revolution once more. Bonaparte has landed on the coast of Provence."'

Blacas, the Minister for War, was immediately sent for. He was inclined to dismiss the invasion as a folly which presented little danger to the throne, but Louis interrupted him impatiently.

'"Blacas, my friend, you are a very pleasant fellow, but that is not enough to make you sensible. You have been wrong on many past occasions, and I am very much afraid that you are once again deluding yourself."'³

Napoleon, in fact, had left Elba on February 26th, 'in extremely calm weather which lasted till March 1st, with 1,000 men or so, aboard a brig and four other vessels, pinks and feluccas.'⁴ Few of the men were thought to be French, they consisted mostly of Poles, Corsicans, Neapolitans and Elbans. He anchored in the Golfe de Juan on March 1st.

The news was all over Paris the day after Louis heard it. Madame de Staël learnt of it, feeling as if the earth were opening to swallow her. Whichever way the invasion went, she felt it would be equally disastrous for France. Meeting Monsieur de Lavelotte shortly afterwards she said to him, 'Liberty is over if Bonaparte triumphs, and national independence is ended if he is defeated.'⁵ She went to the palace to pay her respects to the King, and judged him to be ill at ease behind a façade of courage. 'While leaving the Tuileries, I saw the still unobliterated eagles on the walls of Napoleon's apartments, and they seemed to me to have become threatening again.'⁶

It was another five days before the news was heard in London. It burst upon a public who had almost forgotten Bony's existence in the pressing distresses of the moment, the revolts over the Corn Laws. On the day Napoleon landed in France bread prices fell in Paris to the equivalent of five-pence the quartern loaf, in contrast to a London warning that, if the Corn Bill went through, it would soar there to 1/6d. The price of victory looked unduly high to the poor, who assembled in the streets on the day the bill was to be read, ready to break the windows and doors of the richer citizens. Mary Berry watched them massing under her own windows with alarm. Many of them had come from the Mansion House, where 60,000 signatures had been put to a petition. Hundreds had had to leave without being able to register their protest, because the crowd around the doors was so great. The thwarted populace dispersed, instead, to relieve their feelings by breaking up the houses of members of Parliament—Mr Robinson's in Burlington Street; Lord Darnley's in Berkeley Square; Mr Wellesley-Pole's in Saville Row, and many others. The Earl of Pembroke had his carriage almost broken to pieces about him as he came home from the House of Commons.

On March 11th *The Times* announced the return of Napoleon in a leading article. 'Early yesterday morning we received by express from Dover, the important but lamentable intelligence of a civil war having been again kindled in France by that wretch Bonaparte whose life was so impolitically spared by the Allied Sovereigns. It now appears that the hypo-critical villain, who, at the time of his cowardly abdication, affected an aversion to the shedding of blood in civil warfare, has been employed during the whole of his residence on Elba, in carrying on secret and treasonable intrigues with the tools of his former crimes in France... He will be joined by all the worthless and disaffected, who unhappily form a large portion of the disbanded, and we fear, not a few of the embodied soldiery of France.'[4]

Miss Berry 'could not at first feel alarmed' at the 'fearful news' which immediately wiped the subject of bread from the pages of the Press. She 'could not imagine a nation so degraded, and so stupid as to wish again for a military despotism, after having gone through so dreadful an experience of it.'[6] The invasion at once became the only subject of discussion in the inns and coffee houses. 'Opinions varied wonderfully at the Cocoa Tree.'[7] At first John Cam Hobhouse was the only person there who was willing to bet on Napoleon's success. One habitué had heard that M. Clermont, of the house of Peregaux, swore there was not the least danger for Louis, since the National Guard had declared their loyalty to him. As the week went on, however, coffee house opinion altered and Hobhouse could find nobody willing to back the Bourbons.

Miss Berry had a letter from an English friend in Nice. 'I lose no time in saving you unnecessary anxiety about private individuals. At present we are all tranquillity, and the seat of the disturbance lies not far from this peaceful quarter; but read the following lines, and judge of our consternation.

'The day before yesterday Bonaparte landed at or near Cannes, with 5, 6 or 800 soldiers, and 2 pieces of cannon; he met with no obstacles, but remained quietly on the shore till 11 at night, disembarking with his baggage, ammunition, etc... The flying reports are, that Bonaparte distributes proclamations, saying he is come to the liberation of his faithful subjects, that the eagles are on the wing and will perch from spire to spire, and soon reach those of Notre Dame. He pays any price for horses, and for all other things demanded of him. The Prince of Monaco was detained by a party of Bonaparte's soldiers on his road here; they led him to Bonaparte, who asked him where he was going. "Home," was his reply. "So am I," rejoined the other, and dismissed him... Some people suppose this step to have been taken in desperation; others imagine that it has long been in agitation... The idea of more war sickens all feelings of humanity... One party blame the English for having allowed him to escape—as if the English were to blame. The fact is, our honest *bonhomie* is not done justice to—we are not liked on the continent.'[6]

Paris, in the meanwhile, seemed in a state of stunned inertia, Fanny d'Arblay accurately described the general apathy in recalling her own. 'I have no remembrance how I first heard of the return of Bonaparte from Elba. Wonder at his temerity was the impression made by the news, but wonder unmixed with apprehension. This inactivity of foresight was universal. A torpor indescribable, a species of stupor utterly indefinable, seemed to have enveloped the capital with a mist that was impervious. Everybody went about their affairs, made or received visits, met, and parted, without speaking, or, I suppose, thinking of this event as of a matter of any importance. My own participation in this improvident blindness is to myself incomprehensible. Ten years I had lived under the dominion of Bonaparte; I had been in habits of intimacy with many friends of those who most closely surrounded him;... by narrations the most authentic, and by documents the most indisputable, I knew the character of Bonaparte; and marvellous beyond the reach of my comprehension is my participation in this inertia.'[2]

When the news was brought to Louis most of the French royal family were either absent from Paris or about to leave. The Duc and Duchesse d'Angoulême heard of the invasion from a courier who arrived in the middle of a ball given in their honour by the merchants of Bordeaux. The message required the Duc to proceed at once to Nîmes. The royal couple decided not to spoil the festivities by making the disaster public, and the Duc slipped away at 5 a.m. in a poste chaise. 'Monsieur', the King's brother, had gone to Lyons. The Duc d'Orleans and the Duc de Berri were planning tours of the provinces. The latter, in fact, was actually setting out on the day when the news of Bonaparte's landing became public. His 'horses were harnessed, his trunks tied on, and he had already his foot upon the carriage step, when the buzz was heard to run through the crowd, that the Princes of the Royal Family were abandoning the King, as Louis XVI had been abandoned, and that the Duc de Berri was running away to England. His Royal Highness, upon this, ordered away the equipages, and declared he would remain in Paris, though his destination had been Besançon and the army.'⁴ The Duc d'Orleans set out, with Marshal Ney, to Lyons, prepared to confront the invader.

Louis put a brave face on the situation when he received the diplomatic corps. 'Gentlemen, you see me in pain, but do not deceive yourselves, its cause is not anxiety but the gout. . . . Write to your respective courts that I am well, and that the foolish enterprise of *that man* shall as little disturb the tranquillity of Europe as it has disturbed mine!'⁴ He went to the opera as if nothing had happened and the public shouted for the patriotic song 'Henri IV'. The weather had become foggy, making M. Chappe's telegraphs useless and no news came through of Bonaparte's progress or the lack of it. *The Times* correspondent went to the Place du Carousel to watch the Grand Review of the National Guard and wrote complacently that their enthusiasm for the King had effectually decided Napoleon's fate. Louis, unfortunately, was seized with an excruciating paroxysm of gout at the very moment they marched past his balcony, but this did not prevent the grenadiers from hoisting their caps on their bayonets and making the sky ring with cries of 'Vive le

Roi!' Three days later, at a similar gathering, some of the English still in Paris heard the voices of 'two or three wretches who cried "Vive l'Empereur!"'⁴ These disturbers of the peace were promptly hurried off to the guard house by a posse of gendarmes.

General d'Arblay had been at Senlis, visiting a house where he and Fanny planned to live. On his return the couple at once resumed the 'delightful airings in the Bois de Boulogne'² that had been their habit ever since she had joined him in France. They were not well off, but, since the General had become part of the King's bodyguard, they had permitted themselves the extravagance of a light calèche in which to take the morning air. Their complacency in the face of the menace from the south was not shared by large numbers of English still living in Paris. Remembering the fate of their countrymen who had been *détenus* during the late war, they hastened to equip themselves with passports. Reports were coming in that the country between Paris and Lyons was swarming with deserters hurrying to rejoin their rebel chief, and the danger was that any traveller would be arrested if he were caught on the road without the proper documents. By March 15th crowds were cramming the packet boats or waiting their turn on the quays at Calais, Boulogne and Dieppe.

There was no longer room for doubt that Napoleon was coming steadily nearer, in spite of confident assertions that the towns in his path were all resisting and showing the Bourbon flag. The rapidity of his march was variously explained away as being positively detrimental to his hopes; his forces were small, indifferently armed and presented no real danger; he was weakening himself by advancing so quickly; Marshal Macdonald's retreat was only a 'reculer pour mieux sauter', he was preparing to take Bonaparte in the rear. 'Monsieur' sent cheerful messages. He had been forced to retire from Lyons, but was returning to retake it any moment. Even Wellington, whose disorder in Vienna had turned out to be no more than a tiresome cold, was able to write with guarded optimism. 'Here we are all zeal, and, I think, anxiety to take the field. I moderate these sentiments as much as possible, and get them on paper; and in the meantime am working at a great exertion in case things should become serious in France. But I think the King will settle the business himself, which is the result most to be wished.'⁸

The Press in England was beginning to ask questions. How was it that we, who exerted so much decision and energy in subduing a mob rioting in Westminster over the price of bread, could have allowed the Corsican Viper to land in France unmolested? 'Where was Colonel Campbell? Where were the Russian and Prussian agents? Where were our cruisers? Was it thought *unpolite* to watch the Emperor of Elba?'⁴ Stock Exchange prices slumped in the pervading gloom of the moment, and all officers were ordered back to their regiments in the Netherlands.

It was not until March 16th, more than ten days after news of the crisis had reached it, that Paris realised the peril in which it stood. The King had gone to the Palais Bourbon to make a speech, calm and wearing the ribbon of the Légion d'Honneur. 'Gentlemen, at this critical moment when the public enemy occupies part of my kingdom and menaces the liberty of the rest, I come to you in the desire of strengthening the ties which, by binding you to me, fortify the state. . . I have returned to my country; I have reconciled it with foreign powers which will undoubtedly remain faithful to the treaties which have restored us to peace; I have laboured for the welfare of my people; I have received, I every day receive, most affecting evidences of their love; how could I, at the age of sixty years, better end my existence than by dying in their defence? I fear nothing for myself, but I fear for France.'[1]

As he finished speaking, to cheers from the assembly, the room suddenly darkened. A cloud had come over the sun. A few hours later news was brought that Marshal Ney, who had declared as he left the capital that Napoleon ought to be brought there in an iron cage, had defected to his former master at Lons-le-Saulnier.

Even so, nobody really believed Napoleon would actually enter Paris, though it was plain to everyone that France was in for civil war. Contrary pressures were put on the King, some wishing him to leave the city at once, others, like Marshal Marmont and Chateaubriand, preferring that he should remain in a fortified Tuileries. The papers indignantly repudiated the idea that he would dream of leaving. General d'Arblay, though he remained optimistic until March 18th, had taken the precaution of arming his Fanny with a passport, made out to Madame d'Arblay, née Burney, with no mention of his present situation lest it should impede her escape. Fanny wrote of that day, 'All hope disappeared. From north, from south, from east, from west, alarm took the field, danger flashed its lightnings, and contention growled its thunders; yet in Paris there was no rising, no disturbance, no confusion—all was taciturn suspense, dark dismay, or sullen passiveness.'[2] On the 19th, 'one of the most dreadful days of my existence', her husband came home from two nights on duty, 'harrassed, worn, almost wasted with fatigue', and told her that she would have to leave Paris and that he had arranged for her to go with the Princesse d'Hénin. Fanny sensed his unspoken wish that they should part with outward cheerfulness. They made a short prayer, kneeling together, and separated with smiles and a gay 'Vive le Roi'. She watched from a window, anguish in her heart, as he mounted his horse, which seemed loaded with pistols as if equipped for immediate action on the battlefield. Then she forced herself to prepare, her first instinct being to settle any outstanding debts and pay the rent of their apartment, so that nobody could have any excuse for disposing of their property in her absence. 'The proprietor was thunderstruck by the measure, saying that the King had reiterated his proclamation that he would not desert his capital.'²

It was a dark night and the house of the Princesse d'Hénin was in a turmoil of uncertainty, the ladies doubtful whether to go at once or to wait for further news. The matter was settled when a note came from M. de Lally, announcing that Bonaparte was only a few hours' march from Paris. The Princesse instantly ordered horses to be harnessed to her berlin, and began to take leave of her servants, but word came that no horses were to be had, the Government having put them all in requisition. Eventually one of her old servants managed to persuade a friend from the stables to let her have some for the first stage out of the city. The distracted women at last mounted into the carriage, 'averse, yet eager, between 10 and 11 o'clock'² and drove off into the night.

Earlier the same day, Captain Edmund Walcot, of the Royal Horse Artillery, had walked out on the Place du Carousel and seen the King come in from a drive in his coach-and-eight, followed by a great number of aides-de-camp and cavalry. Walcot had been three days in Paris, staying at the Hôtel Les Puissances Alliées in Rue de la Paix. He had come on a mission to the French Royal Army, but finding the idea of joining it impractical, 'there being only one army and that for Bonaparte', had stayed to see what turn events would take. The sight of Louis seemed to contradict the report that the Royal Family were about to leave. But 'the next morning', he wrote, 'again going to my usual place, the Garden of the Tuileries, I saw the White Flag no longer on top of the Palace. No longer the busy scene of a Palace inhabited by Royalty, but a gloomy appearance of its being deserted, with a straggling sentry here and there. The windows, the day before crowded with soldiers, and the courts, with carriages, gave place to silence and gloom. The fact spoke for itself: the King had left Paris.'⁸ Louis was on his way to Ghent.

It was May 20th. No sooner had the absence of the flag been noticed than the King's pictures, which were in all shop windows, were taken out and replaced by secretly hoarded portraits of the Emperor. White ribbons disappeared and faded red and tricolour ones were taken from the drawers where they lain for a year. At midday the revolutionary flag was hoisted from some of the principal buildings as the advance guard of the invading army reached the city gates.

At nine o'clock, eleven months and two weeks after his abdication, the ex-Emperor, wearing his famous grey overcoat, was carried in triumph up the steps of the Tuileries, where the unremoved emblems of his former rule remained to greet him. The eagles, as he had prophesied, had reached the spires of Notre Dame. Europe was again at war with Napoleon.

NOTES

Chapter I
1. The Times.
2. The Gentleman's Magazine.
3. Extracts from the Journal and Correspondence of Miss Berry. Edited Theresa Lewis. 1866.
4. The Creevey Papers, ed. John Gore. 1963.
5. The Duke. Philip Guedalla. 1931.
6. The Letters of Lady Burghersh. 1893.
7. The Autobiography of Miss Knight. ed. Roger Fulford. 1960.
8. The Diary of Frances, Lady Shelley. ed. Richard Edgcumbe. 1912.
9. The Diary and Letters of Madame d'Arblay. 1842–46.

Chapter II
1. The Times.
2. The Duchesse d'Angoulême and Two Restorations. Imbert de Saint-Amand. Translated James Denis. 1892.
3. A New Picture of Paris. Edward Planta. 1814.
4. Travels in France during the Years 1814–15. Alison and Tytler. 1815.
5. Extracts from the Journal . . . of Miss Berry. 1866.
6. The Gentleman's Magazine.
7. The Duke. Philip Guedalla. 1931.

Chapter III
1. Extracts from the Journal . . . of Miss Berry. 1866.
2. Diary Illustrative of the Times of George IV, interspersed with Letters from Queen Caroline. Lady C. S. M. Campbell, afterwards Lady Bury. 1838.
3. The Times.
4. Travels in France. Alison and Tytler. 1815.
5. Autobiography of Benjamin Robert Haydon. ed. Alex. D. Penrose. 1927.

6. Life of Sir David Wilkie. Allan Cunningham. 1843.
7. Diary of B. R. Haydon. 1960.
8. A Visit to Paris in June 1814. 1814. Henry Wansey.
9. A Tour Through Some Parts of France, etc. Richard Boyle Bernard. 1814.
10. A New Picture of Paris. Edward Planta. 1814.

Chapter IV
1. The Times.
2. The Duchesse d'Angoulême... I. de Saint-Amand. 1892.
3. The Gentleman's Magazine.
4. Extracts from the Journal of Miss Berry. 1866.
5. The Diary of Frances, Lady Shelley. 1912.
6. Diary Illustrative of the Times of George IV. 1838.
7. The Creevey Papers. ed. John Gore. 1963.

Chapter V
1. Autobiography & Journals of B. R. Haydon. 1960.
2. Life of Sir David Wilkie. Allan Cunningham. 1848.
3. A Visit to Paris in June 1814. Henry Wansey. 1814.
4. Journal of a Tour to the Continent. John Mayne. 1909.
5. The Times.
6. Notes on a Journey Through France. Morris Birkbeck. 1814.
7. A Visit to Paris in 1814. John Scott. 1816.
8. Extracts from The Journal of Miss Berry. 1866.

Chapter VI
1. The Times.
2. The Gentleman's Magazine.
3. The Diary of Frances, Lady Shelley. 1912.
4. Diary Illustrative of the Times of George IV. 1838.
5. The Diary & Letters of Madame d'Arblay. 1842–46.
6. Extracts from the Journals ... of Miss Berry. 1866.
7. Private Correspondence, 1781–1821. C. R. Gower, Countess Granville. 1916.

Chapter VII
1. Paris in 1802. William Shepherd. 1814.
2. Journal of a Trip to Paris. John Henry Manners, 5th Duke of Rutland. 1814.
3. Autobiography & Journals of B. R. Haydon. 1960.
4. Life of Sir David Wilkie. Allan Cunningham. 1843.
5. A Visit to Paris in 1814. John Scott. 1816.
6. Correspondence & Table Talk. B. R. Haydon. 1876.
7. The Times.

Chapter VIII
1. The Times.
2. The Diary of Frances, Lady Shelley. 1912.
3. The Gentleman's Magazine.
4. Recollections of a Long Life. Lord Broughton. 1909.

Chapter IX
1. Journal of a Trip to Paris. J. H. Manners. 1814.
2. The Diary & Letters of Madame d'Arblay. 1842–46.
3. The Times.
4. The Duke. Philip Guedalla. 1931.
5. A Visit to Paris in June 1814. Henry Wansey. 1814.
6. Diary of B. R. Haydon. 1960.
7. Life of Sir David Wilkie. Allan Cunningham. 1843.
8. A Visit to Paris in 1814. John Scott. 1814.
9. The Duchesse d'Angoulême... I. de Saint-Amand. 1892.

Chapter X
1. Paris in 1814. William Roots. 1909.
2. The Kembles. P. H. Fitzgerald. 1861.
3. The Times.
4. Diaries, Letters & Reminiscences. H. Crabb Robinson. 1867.
5. Journal of a Tour to the Continent. J. Mayne. 1909.
6. A Visit to Paris in 1814. John Scott. 1816.
7. A Visit to Paris in June 1814. Henry Wansey. 1814.
8. Journal of a Trip to Paris. J. H. Manners. 1814.
9. Life of Sir David Wilkie. Allan Cunningham. 1843.
10. Diary of B. R. Haydon. 1960.
11. Extracts from the Journal of Miss Berry. 1866.

Chapter XI
1. Journal of a Tour to the Continent. John Mayne. 1909.
2. Paris in 1814. William Roots. 1909.
3. The Times.
4. Diaries, Letters & Reminiscences. H. Crabb Robinson. 1867.
5. A Visit to Paris in June 1814. Henry Wansey. 1814.
6. 1815. John Fisher. 1963.
7. Recollections of a Long Life. Lord Broughton. 1909.
8. The Duke. Philip Guedalla. 1931.

Chapter XII
1. The Times.
2. Recollections of a Long Life. Lord Broughton. 1909.

Chapter XIII
1. The Duchesse d'Angoulême . . . I. de Saint Imbert. 1892.
2. The Drawing and Letters of Madame d'Aublay. 1842-46.
3. The Hundred Days. Anthony Brett James. 1964.
4. The Times.
5. The Unpublished Correspondence of Mme de Stael and The Duke of Wellington. ed. Victor Pange. 1965.
6. Extracts from the Journal . . . of Miss Berry. 1866.
7. Recollections of a Long Life. Lord Braughton. 1909.
8. Correspondence of Lady Burghersh with the Duke of Wellington. 1903.

Index